Sharon V.
KRAMER

Mike
MATTOS

Austin
BUFFUM

BEST
Practices
at Tier 2

Supplemental
Interventions
for Additional
Student Support

Secondary

Solution Tree | Press a division of
Solution Tree

555 North Morton Street
Bloomington, IN 47404
800.733.6786 (toll free) / 812.336.7700
FAX: 812.336.7790

email: info@SolutionTree.com
SolutionTree.com

Visit **go.SolutionTree.com/RTIatWork** to download the free reproducibles in this book.

Printed in the United States of America

Library of Congress Cataloging-in-Publication Data

Names: Sonju, Bob, 1967- author.
Title: Best practices at tier 2 : supplemental interventions for additional
   student support, secondary / Bob Sonju, Sharon V. Kramer, Mike Mattos, and
   Austin Buffum.
Other titles: Best practices at tier two
Description: Bloomington, IN : Solution Tree Press, 2019. | Includes
   bibliographical references and index.
Identifiers: LCCN 2018055485 | ISBN 9781942496847 (perfect bound)
Subjects: LCSH: Remedial teaching--United States. | Individualized
   instruction--United States. | Response to intervention (Learning disabled
   children)--United States. | Learning disabled children--Education
   (Secondary)--United States.
Classification: LCC LB1029.R4 S66 2019 | DDC 371.9--dc23 LC record available at https://lccn.loc
   .gov/2018055485

Solution Tree
Jeffrey C. Jones, CEO
Edmund M. Ackerman, President

Solution Tree Press
President and Publisher: Douglas M. Rife
Associate Publisher: Sarah Payne-Mills
Art Director: Rian Anderson
Managing Production Editor: Kendra Slayton
Senior Production Editor: Christine Hood
Content Development Specialist: Amy Rubenstein
Copy Editor: Evie Madsen
Proofreader: Kate St. Ives
Text and Cover Designer: Jill Resh
Editorial Assistant: Sarah Ludwig

I dedicate this book to my colleagues who are passionately committed to thinking differently, willing to challenge the educational norm, and truly doing what is best for all students.

—Bob Sonju

I would like to dedicate this book to the people who call me Mom and Grandma. They are the reason and inspiration for this work and the true measure of my success.

—Sharon V. Kramer

I dedicate this book to my first principal and dear friend, Dr. Marilyn Kemple. Thank you for hiring a rookie social studies teacher, allowing me to take chances, and for modeling that good is never good enough.

—Mike Mattos

I dedicate this book to the two lighthouses that guided my adult life: Dr. Donald Cole and Dr. Richard DuFour.

—Austin Buffum

Acknowledgments

The authors of this book met due to our common belief that the PLC at Work® process is the best way to ensure learning for both students and educators. Certainly, this book represents the power of collaboration. We would like to thank Jeffrey Jones, Douglas Rife, and the amazing professionals at Solution Tree for their support of this project. It was Douglas who proposed we write a collaborative series on best instructional practices at each tier of the RTI process. Christine Hood did an outstanding job of editing this book. We feel so fortunate to work with a company that is truly committed to achieving their vision of transforming education worldwide to ensure learning for all.

We are eternally grateful to the original authors of the PLC at Work process: Richard DuFour, Rebecca DuFour, and Robert Eaker. Their mentorship, friendship, and support over the years have transformed our thinking about best practice and serves as the foundation of our RTI at Work approach to systematic interventions.

I would like to thank Mike Mattos and Austin Buffum for their dedication to the students who need us the most. They have always approached this important work in a practical and no-nonsense manner. Over the years, their efforts have changed the lives of students worldwide. I would also like to thank Bob Sonju for his ability to approach the writing of this book with an open mind and a can-do attitude. He made this entire process much easier and enjoyable.

—Sharon V. Kramer

We would like to thank our co-authors, Sharon V. Kramer and Bob Sonju, as they wrote a vast majority of this book. For them, the PLC at Work framework and RTI process are not theories, for they have lived both and gained the type of first-hand, practical knowledge that can only be acquired through doing the work at a very high level. They have been recognized as outstanding classroom teachers, site administrators, and district leaders. Both have led model PLC at Work schools and districts, advised state and national policymakers, and helped schools around the world. We are exceedingly grateful to Sharon and Bob for their willingness to take on this project and for their efforts to connect their expertise and ideas to our RTI at Work process.

—Austin Buffum and Mike Mattos

I'd be remiss if I didn't thank my mom and dad for teaching me to work and care; Mike Mattos for his mentorship and example; Austin Buffum for his wisdom; Sharon Kramer for her extensive expertise and patience in blending our thoughts and voices (as well as the many laughs); and of course, the Solution Tree editors and staff for bringing this project together into one complete resource. Most of all, I want to thank Leslye and my girls; there are simply not words sufficient enough to describe how much I love you.

—Bob Sonju

Solution Tree Press would like to thank the following reviewers:

Matthew Blackmore
Principal
Carlisle High School
Carlisle, Iowa

Kari Murray
Building Learning Coordinator
Carlisle High School
Carlisle, Iowa

Kimberly Calcasola
Assistant Principal
Granby Memorial High School
Granby, Connecticut

Jacqueline Price
English and Composition Teacher
Franklin High School
Livonia, Michigan

Isaac McCord
Principal
Western Oaks Middle School
Bethany, Oklahoma

Visit **go.SolutionTree.com/RTIatWork**
to download the free reproducibles in this book.

Table of Contents

Reproducibles are in italics.

About the Authors

 **Bob Sonju** is an award-winning educational leader and consultant recognized for his energetic commitment to building effective teams, developing response to intervention (RTI) structures that support teachers and students, and creating effective school cultures committed to student learning. He is executive director of learning and development for Washington County School District and a former adjunct professor of education at Dixie State University in Utah. Bob was formerly the principal of U.S.-recognized Fossil Ridge Intermediate School and has also served as a district leader, high school administrator, and special education teacher.

Together with his staff, Bob helped Fossil Ridge develop into a true a professional learning community (PLC) that continues to produce extraordinary results. Fossil Ridge was selected as a 2013 (and 2016) National Breakthrough School by the National Association of Secondary School Principals. Their work as a school has been featured in on http://AllThingsPLC.info and in *Principle Leadership Magazine* Bob is leading the implementation of the PLC process in a district composed of fifty schools.

Utah Association of Secondary School Principals named Bob 2011 Principal of the Year for middle-level schools, and the National Association of Secondary School Principals selected him as one of three finalists for National Principal of the Year. His work has been published in *Principal Leadership Magazine*, *Impact Journal*, and *It's About Time*.

Bob earned a bachelor's degree, a master's degree, and an endorsement in school administration from Southern Utah University.

 **Sharon V. Kramer, PhD,** knows firsthand the demands and rewards of working in a professional learning community. As a leader in the field, she emphasizes the importance of creating and using quality assessments as a continual part of the learning process. Sharon served as assistant superintendent for curriculum and instruction of Kildeer Countryside Community Consolidated School District 96 in Illinois. In this position, she ensured all students were prepared to enter Adlai E. Stevenson High School, a model PLC started and formerly led by Richard DuFour.

A seasoned educator, Sharon has taught in elementary and middle school classrooms and served as principal, director of elementary education, and university professor. In addition to her PLC experience, Sharon has completed assessment training by Rick Stiggins, Steve Chappuis, Larry Ainsworth, and the Center for Performance Assessment (now the Leadership and Learning Center). She has presented a variety of assessment workshops at institutes and summits and for state departments of education. Sharon has also worked with school districts across the United States to determine their power standards and develop assessments.

She has been a Comprehensive School Reform consultant to schools that have received grant funding to implement PLC as their whole-school reform model, and her customized PLC coaching academies have empowered school and district leadership teams across the United States. Sharon has presented at state and national conferences sponsored by Learning Forward, National Association for Gifted Children, American Federation of Teachers, and California State University. She has been instrumental in facilitating professional development initiatives focused on standards-based learning and teaching, improved understanding and utilization of assessment data, interventions and differentiation that meet the needs of all learners, and strengthened efforts to ensure K–12 literacy.

Sharon is also the author of *How to Leverage PLCs for School Improvement* and co-author of *School Improvement for ALL: A How-to Guide for Doing the Right Work.* She also contributed to the books *It's About Time: Planning Interventions and Extensions in Elementary School, The Teacher as Assessment Leader,* and *The Collaborative Teacher: Working Together as a Professional Learning Community.*

Sharon earned a doctorate in educational leadership and policy studies from Loyola University Chicago.

To learn more about Sharon's work, follow her @DrKramer1 on Twitter.

Mike Mattos is an internationally recognized author, presenter, and practitioner who specializes in uniting teachers, administrators, and support staff to transform schools by implementing the response to intervention and PLC processes. Mike co-created the RTI at Work model, which builds on the foundation of the PLC at Work framework by using team structures and a focus on learning, collaboration, and results to drive successful outcomes and creating a systematic, multitiered system of supports to ensure high levels of learning for all students. He is former principal of Marjorie Veeh Elementary School and Pioneer Middle School in California. At both schools, Mike helped create powerful PLCs, improving learning for all students.

In 2004, Marjorie Veeh, an elementary school with a large population of youth at risk, won the California Distinguished School and National Title I Achieving School awards. A National Blue Ribbon School, Pioneer is among only thirteen schools in the United States that the GE Foundation selected as a Best-Practice Partner and is one of eight schools that Richard DuFour chose to feature in the video series *The Power of Professional Learning Communities at Work: Bringing the Big Ideas to Life*. Based on standardized test scores, Pioneer ranks among the top 1 percent of California secondary schools and, in 2009 and 2011, was named Orange County's top middle school.

For his leadership, Mike was named the Orange County Middle School Administrator of the Year by the Association of California School Administrators. Mike has coauthored many other books focused on response to intervention and professional learning communities, including *Learning by Doing: A Handbook for Professional Learning Communities at Work*; *Concise Answers to Frequently Asked Questions About Professional Learning Communities at Work*; *Simplifying Response to Intervention: Four Essential Guiding Principles*; *Pyramid Response to Intervention: RTI, Professional Learning Communities, and How to Respond When Kids Don't Learn*; *Uniting Academic and Behavior Interventions: Solving the Skill or Will Dilemma*; *It's About Time: Planning Interventions and Extensions in Secondary School*; *It's About Time: Planning Interventions and Extensions in Elementary School*; *Best Practices at Tier 1: Daily Differentiation for Effective Instruction, Secondary*; *Best Practices at Tier 1: Daily Differentiation for Effective Instruction, Elementary*; and *The Collaborative Administrator: Working Together as a Professional Learning Community*.

To learn more about Mike's work, visit AllThingsPLC (www.allthingsplc.info) and http://mattos.info/welcome.html, or follow him @mikemattos65 on Twitter.

Austin Buffum, EdD, has forty-seven years of experience in public schools. His many roles include serving as former senior deputy superintendent of California's Capistrano Unified School District. Austin has presented in over nine hundred school districts throughout the United States and around the world. He delivers trainings and presentations on the RTI at Work model. This tiered approach to response to intervention is centered on PLC at Work concepts and strategies to ensure every student receives the time and support necessary to succeed.

Austin also delivers workshops and presentations that provide the tools educators need to build and sustain PLCs. Austin was selected 2006 Curriculum and Instruction Administrator of the Year by the Association of California School Administrators. He attended the Principals' Center at the Harvard Graduate School of Education and was greatly inspired by its founder, Roland Barth, an early advocate of the collaborative culture that defines PLCs today. He later led Capistrano's K–12 instructional program on an increasingly collaborative path toward operating as a PLC. During this process, thirty-seven of the district's schools were designated California Distinguished Schools, and eleven received National Blue Ribbon recognition.

Austin is coauthor with Suzette Lovely of *Generations at School: Building an Age-Friendly Learning Community*. He has also coauthored *Uniting Academic and Behavior Interventions: Solving the Skill or Will Dilemma*; *It's About Time: Planning Interventions and Extensions in Elementary School*; *It's About Time: Planning Interventions and Extensions in Secondary School*; *Simplifying Response to Intervention: Four Essential Guiding Principles*; and *Pyramid Response to Intervention: RTI, Professional Learning Communities, and How to Respond When Kids Don't Learn*.

A graduate of the University of Southern California, Austin earned a bachelor of music degree and received a master of education degree with honors. He holds a doctor of education degree from Nova Southeastern University.

To learn more about Austin's work, follow him @agbuffum on Twitter.

To book Bob Sonju, Sharon V. Kramer, Mike Mattos, or Austin Buffum for professional development, contact pd@SolutionTree.com.

Introduction

Throughout life, we often determine our actions using three criteria: (1) things we must do, (2) things we need to do, and (3) things we want to do. First are things we *must* do. Regardless of our own personal preferences and opinions, a higher authority has deemed a specific action mandatory, and punitive repercussions are usually applied if we fail to comply. An obvious example of a *must* do is paying taxes. A property tax bill is not a suggestion, a recommendation, or a donation. Even if we philosophically disagree with the government's authority to collect taxes, or the specifics of the tax code, all citizens must pay their taxes or face the consequences.

The second criteria that guides our actions are things that we *need* to do. *Need to do* actions include those we deem important, regardless of personal likes or dislikes. An example of this might be eating a balanced diet. While no law states we must meet daily governmental dietary guidelines, most people would agree that eating more fruits and vegetables and cutting down on processed sugars and saturated fats is best for long-term health. The thing about a *need to do* action is that just because we believe we *should* do an action, there is no guarantee we will actually do it.

Finally, there are things that we *want* to do. We are motivated to do these things by more than the logic of a likely benefit. Instead, an internal desire drives us. As children, our individual likes influence our wants, such as, "I like cookies, so I think I'll eat one or two or ten." But as we mature, our values, commitments, and experiences deeply influence our wants. Consider a new parent getting up in the middle of the night to feed a crying baby. There is no law requiring parents to feed a newborn in the middle of the night, but if you have been that parent, you know you are drawn from your bed by more than logic or guilt. There is a deeper, internal desire to sooth and protect your child. You might not *like* getting up at 2 a.m., but you *want* to help your baby.

Decisions in life become harder when there is conflict between what we *must* do, what we *need* to do, and what we *want* to do. For example, "I really need to work out, but I'd rather sit on the couch and watch TV." Likewise, we make our easiest decisions when an action aligns to all three criteria—what we are required to do is something we believe we need to do, and we would want to do it, regardless of the external mandate.

As educators, we use these three criteria in our professional lives. For example, let's apply them to the central topic of this book: response to intervention (RTI).

The Three Criteria and RTI

Also commonly referred to as a multitiered system of supports (MTSS), RTI has been federally mandated in the United States since the last reauthorization of special education (Individuals With Disabilities Education Improvement Act [IDEIA], 2004). Each state has subsequently written regulations with specific implementation guidelines. For U.S. schools receiving federal or state funding, RTI is a *must* do. Subsequently, many schools approach RTI implementation like paying their taxes; they begrudgingly offer the very minimum required and look for loopholes around the work when possible. Approaching RTI with this minimalist, defensive attitude is unlikely to inspire the faculty or significantly improve student learning.

The purpose of RTI is to create a systematic process to ensure *every* student receives the additional time and support needed to learn at high levels, as *Simplifying Response to Intervention* (Buffum, Mattos, & Weber, 2012) notes:

> RTI's underlying premise is that schools should not delay providing help for struggling students until they fall far enough behind to qualify for special education, but instead should provide timely, targeted, systematic interventions to all students who demonstrate the need. (p. xiii)

Virtually every school has students who would benefit from additional help, and it is unrealistic to expect individual teachers—working in isolation—to meet the diverse needs of all the students assigned to his or her classroom. Based on these undeniable facts, most educators see the *need* to provide systematic interventions in their school.

To achieve this goal, educators should implement the practices proven to be most effective. When it comes to how schools should structure systematic interventions, the research and evidence have never been more conclusive—RTI is the most effective way to intervene. Educator and researcher John Hattie (2018) completed the most comprehensive meta-analysis on the prevailing research on RTI and finds an outstanding 1.29 standard deviation rate per school year. To put this in perspective, Hattie equates a 1.0 impact rate to a two to three grade-level growth in a single school year (Hattie, 2009). Schools are expected to ensure every student succeeds, so the need to implement RTI is undeniable.

But like improving your diet, just acknowledging the need is not sufficient to ensure you actually commit to *doing* it. Changing your diet impacts more than a lone meal, a single day, or a few weeks; it requires an everyday, ongoing lifestyle change. Implementing RTI successfully is no different, and this level of change is hard. Overwhelmed by the day-to-day demands of the job and overburdened with layers of *must* do reform initiatives, it is not surprising that many well-intentioned educators find it difficult to fully commit to implementing RTI.

However, we have had the distinct honor of working with schools fully committed to the RTI process—they *want* to do it! They embrace the need and would continue the practices regardless of federal, state, and local mandates. These schools did not develop this desire prior to starting RTI implementation, but instead, *during* implementation. Most people become committed to something once they see that it works. While undoubtedly some staff members at these schools began their RTI journey viewing it as a mandate, they committed when they saw evidence of their efforts helping more students learn. Positive results drive their powerful transition from *must* do to *want* to. Unless a school drives its RTI efforts for improving student learning, instead of merely complying to mandates, it is unlikely the faculty will ever fully commit to the process. And improving the achievement of struggling students requires effective interventions.

The Importance of Effective Interventions

To create a systematic, multitiered intervention process, a school must develop some big-picture, schoolwide processes and structures. For example, because RTI requires staff collaboration, the formation of essential teams—teacher teams, a (site) leadership team, and an intervention team—is necessary. The school must schedule time within the contractual day for team collaboration, and teams must dedicate intervention time within the master schedule. The school must create timely processes for schoolwide identification of students in need of help and identify staff to lead specific interventions. These considerations are necessary building blocks that create the school's systematic response when students need additional time and support.

But equally important, a system of interventions is only as effective as its individual interventions (Buffum et al., 2012). If a school builds a system of interventions with ineffective instructional practices, all students will have access to what is not working. Ineffective interventions not only fail students but also the faculty, who will get frustrated because their commitment does not result in student improvement and success. Without results, staff commitment will wane, and they will view future efforts as a must do at best.

Therefore, the purpose of this book is to provide specific, proven instructional practices and processes to improve a school's Tier 2 supplemental interventions. But before we dig deeply into these practices, it is critical to build clarity on some essential vocabulary, starting with what we mean by *Tier 2* and how it fits into a larger MTSS.

The RTI at Work Pyramid

After working with hundreds of schools and districts around the world, we have found that many use RTI jargon, coupled with a general lack of specificity on what the terminology means. With this in mind, we have carefully rethought and revised the traditional RTI pyramid. We refer to our visual framework as the *RTI at Work pyramid*, as shown in figure I.1. We call it *RTI at Work* because it leverages research-based processes to ensure student learning—professional learning communities and RTI.

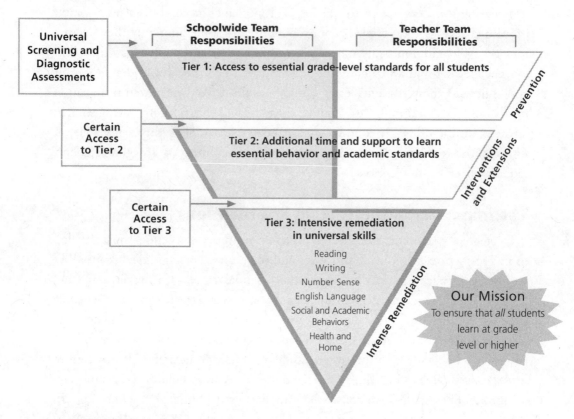

Source: Buffum, Mattos, & Malone, 2018, p. 18.

Figure I.1: The RTI at Work pyramid.

At first glance, you will probably notice our pyramid is upside down. This is because we find some educators misinterpret the traditional RTI pyramid as a new way to qualify students for special education. States, provinces, and school districts visually reinforce this conclusion when they place special education at the top of the pyramid, as shown in figure I.2.

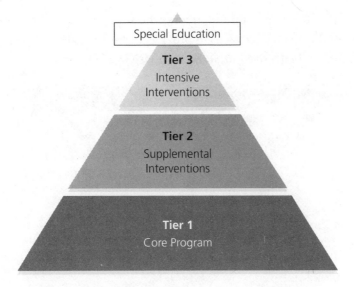

Source: Buffum et al., 2018, p. 19.

Figure I.2: RTI pyramid with special education at the top.

To challenge this negative view of the traditional pyramid, we inverted it to create the RTI at Work pyramid (see figure I.1, page 4), so we could focus interventions on a single point—each individual student. See figure I.3.

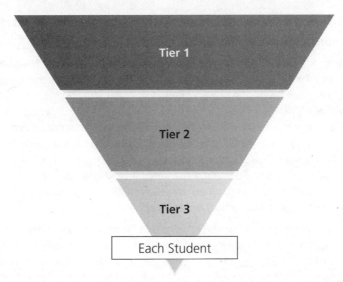

Source: Buffum et al., 2018, p. 19.

Figure I.3: Inverted RTI at Work pyramid.

The widest part of the pyramid represents the school's core instruction program. The purpose of this tier—*Tier 1*—is to provide *all* students access to essential grade-level curriculum and effective initial teaching (see figure I.4).

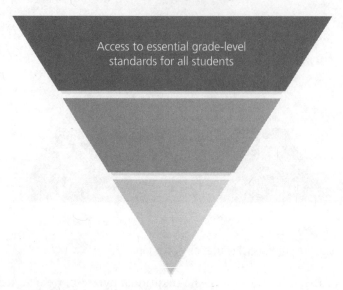

Access to essential grade-level standards for all students

Source: Buffum et al., 2018, p. 20.

Figure I.4: Tier 1 represents the core instruction program.

As we state in *Taking Action: A Handbook for RTI at Work* (Buffum et al., 2018), our most comprehensive book on RTI:

> Many traditional RTI approaches advocate that the key to Tier 1 is effective first instruction. We don't disagree with this, but this teaching must include instruction on the skills, knowledge, and behaviors that a student must acquire during the current year to be prepared for following year. Unfortunately, many schools deem their most at-risk students incapable of learning grade-level curriculum, so they pull out these students and place them in Tier 3 interventions that replace core instruction with remedial coursework. So, even if the initial teaching is done well, if a student's core instruction is focused on below-grade-level standards, then he or she will learn well below grade level.
>
> If the fundamental purpose of RTI is to ensure all students learn at high levels—grade level or better each year—then we must teach students at grade level. Every student might not leave each school year having mastered *every* grade-level standard, but he or she must master the learning outcomes deemed indispensable for future success. (pp. 20–21)

There is a time in every unit of study when *most* students learn the unit's essential learning outcomes, and the teacher must move on to the next unit. But, undoubtedly, some students will not have mastered these outcomes, and the school must provide additional support to these students *without missing critical new core instruction*. This supplemental support is the purpose of Tier 2. See figure I.5.

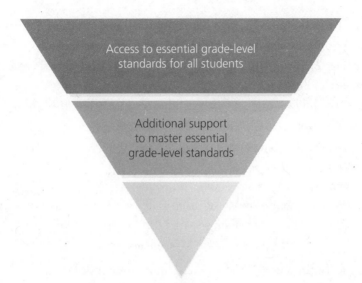

Source: *Buffum et al., 2018, p. 21.*

Figure I.5: Tier 2 interventions provide students supplemental help to master grade-level curriculum.

Tier 2 is a critical point and the focus of this book. Traditional RTI approaches often define Tier 2 by either the size of the intervention group or the duration of the intervention. This approach has limitations when applied across all grades and subjects. Instead, we believe the targeted learning outcomes are the defining characteristic of Tier 2. Supplemental help should primarily focus on providing struggling students with the additional time and support they need to master the specific skills, knowledge, and behaviors identified at Tier 1 to be absolutely essential for future success.

As *Taking Action* (Buffum et al., 2018) notes:

> Classroom teacher teams should be actively involved at Tier 2, as these outcomes directly relate to their areas of expertise. Because supplemental interventions are focused on very specific learning targets, placement into Tier 2 interventions must be timely, targeted, flexible, and most often guided by team-created common assessments aligned to grade-level essential standards. (p. 21)

Equally important, students who do master essential curriculum during core instruction can use Tier 2 time to extend their learning. To be clear, there is an important difference between *enrichment* and *extension*. Teachers use *extension* activities to stretch students beyond essential grade-level curriculum or levels of proficiency. Teachers use *enrichment* activities to provide students with access to the subjects that specials or electives teachers traditionally teach, such as music, art, drama, applied technology, and physical education. This curriculum is essential for all students (Buffum et al., 2018). Teachers should use Tier 2 time for extension, not enrichment.

If students receive essential grade-level curriculum and effective initial teaching during Tier 1 core instruction, and targeted supplemental supports in meeting the standards at Tier 2, then most students should be successful. But there are undoubtedly students who enter school without the foundational skills needed to learn at high levels. According to *Taking Action* (Buffum et al., 2018), these foundation skills include the ability to:

1. Decode and comprehend grade-level text
2. Write effectively
3. Apply number sense
4. Comprehend the English language (or the school's primary language)
5. Consistently demonstrate social and academic behaviors
6. Overcome complications due to health and home (p. 22)

According to Buffum et al. (2018), these foundational skills:

> Enable a student to comprehend instruction, access information, demonstrate understanding, and behave appropriately in a school setting. If a student is significantly behind in just one of these universal skills, he or she will struggle in virtually every grade level, course, and subject. And usually a school's most at-risk students are behind in more than one area. Therefore, for students who need intensive remediation in foundational skills, the school must have a plan to provide this level of assistance *without denying these students access to grade-level essential curriculum*. This is the purpose of Tier 3. (p. 22)

See figure I.6.

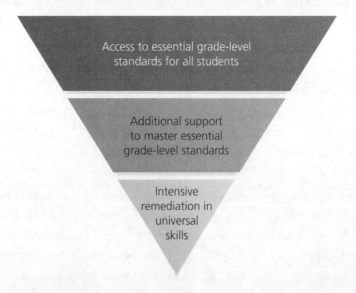

Source: Buffum et al., 2018, p. 22.

Figure I.6: Tier 3 interventions provide intensive remediation in foundational skills.

Because students develop foundational skills over time, schools must provide intensive interventions for struggling students during the instructional day. Highly trained staff should lead these interventions in a student's targeted areas of need.

Finally, RTI is considered a multitiered process because some students need *all three tiers* to learn at high levels. Tiers are cumulative. All students need effective initial instruction on grade-level essential standards at Tier 1; *and* some students need additional time and support in meeting grade-level essential standards at Tier 2—the focus of this book. And in addition to Tier 1 and Tier 2, some students need intensive help in learning essential outcomes from previous years, the purpose of Tier 3.

Individual teachers cannot offer this level of support alone. Instead, it requires a schoolwide, collaborative effort in which the entire staff takes collective responsibility for student learning. It also requires ongoing collaborative processes to create a guaranteed and viable curriculum and common formative assessments to target Tier 2 interventions. This is why structuring a school to function as a PLC is the key to effectively implementing RTI.

To make this point as explicit as possible, *being a PLC is an essential prerequisite to successful RTI implementation.* Specifically, we advocate for the PLC at Work framework first created by Richard DuFour and Robert Eaker (1998). The essential characteristics of the PLC at Work process are perfectly aligned with the fundamental elements of RTI. PLCs and RTI are complementary processes, built on a proven research base of best practices and designed to produce the same outcome—high levels of student learning. PLCs create the foundation required to build a highly effective system of interventions. The guiding principles to this foundation are captured in the three big ideas of the PLC at Work process: (1) a focus on learning, (2) a collaborative culture, and (3) a results orientation.

Additionally, the following four critical questions guide the work of collaborative teams in a PLC (DuFour et al., 2016):

1. What do students need to know and be able to do?
2. How will we know when they have learned it?
3. How will we respond if they haven't learned it?
4. How will we extend the learning for those who already know it? (p. 251)

For schools functioning as a PLC, RTI research can provide a structure to answer the third and fourth critical questions. While this book includes many references to the PLC process, for a deeper dive into more specifics, we highly recommend the book *Learning by Doing* (DuFour, DuFour, Eaker, Many, & Mattos, 2016).

When Tier 1 instruction is not enough for some students to grasp the content, that's when teams offer Tier 2 interventions. These powerful strategies and supports can help students get back on track before they fall further behind.

The Power of Effective Tier 2 Interventions

The short- and long-term benefits of effective Tier 2 interventions across all the tiers of the RTI process are profound. Most essential standards are not isolated skills or content. Teachers teach these standards over many units of study through carefully designed learning progressions. Failing to master a specific step in a sequence can cripple a student's ability to succeed in subsequent core instruction. The longer this continues, the less the student will benefit from new Tier 1 instruction.

However, if this student receives timely, effective Tier 2 interventions, his or her success in new Tier 1 instruction increases, while the need for additional supplemental interventions decreases. Additionally, when more students enter a school year with the prerequisite skills and behaviors for the new grade-level curriculum, core teachers will need to spend less time reteaching the prior year's curriculum. This allows more Tier 1 time to focus on the new required curriculum.

In the long term, when more students master the essential curriculum needed for success in the next grade or course, fewer students will need Tier 3 intensive remediation in subsequent years. Considering that most schools struggle with having enough personnel and resources to implement RTI, decreasing the number of students in need of interventions allows a school to reallocate precious intervention resources to the remaining students in need of additional support. It also means fewer students will drop so far below grade level that their achievement discrepancy might lead to potential special education identification—a process that is time consuming, costly, and traditionally often biased toward male students, minorities, and children of poverty (U.S. Department of Education, 2006).

When implemented correctly, Tier 2 interventions can be key to helping students get back on track to academic success. However, teachers and teams must be sure to avoid common mistakes in implementation.

Common Tier 2 Implementation Mistakes

Effective Tier 2 interventions support the proverbial "an ounce of prevention is worth a pound of cure" situation (Goodreads, n.d.). With such substantial benefits, why are so many schools struggling to realize these outcomes? In 2015, the National Center for Education Evaluation and Regional Assistance released a federally funded study on RTI (Balu et al., 2015). The study identifies the following three significant implementation errors that decrease RTI effectiveness.

1. **Students receiving supplemental intervention often miss new essential core curriculum:** Sixty-nine percent of schools in the study offered at least some intervention services during Tier 1 core instruction, noting: "In such schools, intervention may have displaced instruction time and replaced some small-group or other instruction services with intervention services. As a result, reading intervention services may have been different from, but not necessarily supplemental to, core reading instruction" (Balu et al., 2015, p. ES-11).

   A basic tenet of RTI is that schools should provide interventions in addition to effective Tier 1 core instruction, not in place of it. Our on-site experiences demonstrate that most schools have not engaged their faculty in creating a guaranteed and viable curriculum, so the staff do not have clarity on the specific essential standards students can't miss to receive interventions. It is impossible to ensure all students have access to essential grade-level curriculum outcomes if the faculty can't articulate exactly which standards all students must learn for future success. Additionally, many schools have not allocated specific time in the master schedule for Tier 2 interventions during which teachers will not deliver new essential core curriculum at Tier 1.

2. **Schools use assessments inaccurately:** The study (Balu et al., 2015) finds the most common implementation of RTI is fairly rigid, with schools often using a single test to identify students for Tier 2 (Sparks, 2015). If the purpose of Tier 2 is to reteach essential standards or specific learning targets that make up a larger essential standard, then what single assessment can schools give at the start of the year to determine the exact standards specific students will not master after receiving Tier 1 core instruction? Such an assessment tool does not exist. Most schools and districts have not engaged their faculty in the PLC process in which teacher teams identify essential curriculum and create common assessments directly aligned to those standards, so they cannot identify students in need of Tier 2 help by student or by standard.

   In place of team common assessments, schools are using universal screening assessments, prior-year state assessment data, district benchmark assessments, or report card grades to identify and place students in Tier 2 interventions. These assessments measure broad foundational skills, prior-year curriculum, or large blocks of the core curriculum—not the essential curriculum in a specific unit of Tier 1 core instruction.

3. **Staff demonstrate a lack of collective responsibility for student learning:** Balu et al. (2015) find that in 37 percent of the schools, "classroom teachers played an additional role and provided intervention services" (p. ES-11). RTI advocates that staff members with a higher level of expertise in a student's target area of need should be the ones providing the interventions. Applying this criterion, which staff members would be best prepared to help fifth-grade students struggling with a fifth-grade essential reading standard? The fifth-grade teacher team! And which staff members would be best trained to help students struggling with a specific biology essential standard? Biology teachers, of course!

   Because Tier 2 focuses on reteaching the essential core curriculum, teacher teams should be heavily involved in Tier 2 interventions. But the key here is the word *team*. In many schools, some teachers keep their own students for Tier 2 interventions, and rarely do they save their best instructional practices for these interventions. More often, teachers provide students with the same pedagogies from core instruction, only in smaller group settings.

Along with the three mistakes the study (Balu et al., 2015) identifies, we have identified two more through our work with schools.

1. **Some schools or districts rely too heavily on purchased intervention products to provide Tier 2 interventions:** There are a couple of significant drawbacks to these programs. First, there is no guarantee that the curricular focus of the product aligns with team-identified essential standards. When this is the case, teachers tend to let the intervention program drive their Tier 1 curriculum instruction. Second, multiple students can struggle on the same essential standard but not for the same reason. Many intervention programs lack the ability to accurately diagnose *why* a student fails to learn. There are some very good, scientific research-based products available that can become powerful, targeted tools in a school's intervention toolbox— but there is no single solution for all students who struggle.

2. **Many schools perpetuate ineffective instructional practices:** When we work with schools, we often have staff list their current site interventions. Commonly, Tier 2 lists include things like lunchtime or after-school help, study halls, the resource room, instructional aides, and in-class flexible groupings. These are all interventions research concludes are generally ineffective (Buffum et al., 2012; Hattie, 2009). When it comes to interventions, giving students at risk more

of what is not working is not the answer. Common sense tells us this, yet many schools continue to build their intervention systems with practices that don't work, have never worked, and have no promise of getting better results the following year (Buffum et al., 2012).

In this book, you will learn about how to avoid these mistakes as well as discover effective strategies and tools for implementing Tier 2 supports to help all students learn at high levels.

In This Book

This book is written for practitioners by practitioners. It is part of a three-book series on best instructional practices for each tier of the RTI process.

The interventions in this book focus on ongoing processes, not programs, in Tier 2 supports. These processes are grounded in proven instructional practices and applicable in virtually all grade levels and subjects, and for all student demographics.

Simply stated, the intent of Tier 2 intervention is to provide additional time and support beyond initial instruction to prevent students from falling behind. We have a profound desire to help schools and teams become more effective in providing Tier 2 targeted intervention to help all students learn at high levels. Through extensive experiences (both good and sometimes not so good), research, and best practice, we have discovered both cultural and structural practices that strengthen learning, support teams, and lead to high levels of learning for every student. Throughout this book, you will see a clear structure for each chapter divided into the following four sections.

▽ **Why We Need to Do Things Differently:** Each chapter presents research and practical examples to build a compelling case for doing things differently.

▽ **Here's How:** Each chapter provides templates, practical strategies, and real-school examples of what effective Tier 2 interventions look like in schools that have been successful.

▽ **Big Ideas:** After the Conclusion of each chapter, we share the chapter's big ideas. These big ideas should serve as the critical points for you and your teams to consider when planning your next steps.

▽ **Key Considerations Rubric:** Designed to assess your team or school's current reality, each chapter concludes with statements in a reproducible rubric. These statements are designed to guide your school or team thinking and stimulate deep conversations as you move forward.

As we look forward, each chapter of this book will focus on select foundational principles of effective Tier 2 interventions. Each of these foundational principles is essential as schools create targeted time and support for students.

Chapter 1 makes a case for working in highly effective teams and the *why* behind the need to identify essential standards (a guaranteed and viable curriculum). It also explains why teams must use common formative assessments that target specific skills, allowing teams to intervene more effectively.

Chapter 2 clarifies the difference among Tier 1 initial instruction, Tier 2 supplemental interventions, and Tier 3 intensive remediation. It also defines the roles for each team (teacher teams, leadership team, and an intervention team) essential to building an effective intervention structure, along with ideas for who could be included on each team.

Chapter 3 begins to get to the *how* of Tier 2 interventions. It focuses on processes that help teams identify essential standards and deconstruct standards into measurable learning targets. This shared clarity in the standards and targets leads to Tier 2 interventions that are targeted on specific skills.

Usable data is a critical component of an effective intervention structure. Chapter 4 discusses strategies for using the correct kind of data to help teams identify students who require additional time and support.

Chapter 5 introduces a variety of instructional supports for students. From implementing re-engagement strategies to ideas for extending the learning of those who are already proficient, teams will find lots of ideas as they consider implementing Tier 2 interventions.

Chapter 6 offers readers a variety of ways to build targeted Tier 2 interventions into their daily schedules. It showcases a variety of secondary schools that have created ways to provide extra time within their daily schedules to provide interventions. It shares each school's schedule and structures to help kick start your thinking as you create systems of support at your school.

Our goal is to provide detailed descriptions, strategies, and example scenarios from real schools (with fictitious names) that make a significant difference in providing additional time and support and, in turn, ensure each student in your school learns at high levels. The information in this book is a compilation of research, best practices, and just some plain great ideas we have seen work. These ideas are meant to encourage your own school's collective thinking regarding Tier 2 intervention and high levels of learning for *all* students.

Most of all, the ideas in this book will assist you and your school as you begin (or continue) the conversation and make changes focused on student learning and critical Tier 2 time and support. These conversations and changes are the beginning of a transformation from *the way we've always done things around here* to discovering a new collective purpose and strategically utilizing time within the school day to provide students with the Tier 2 interventions they will need to learn.

These interventions should not require hiring additional staff, buying additional resources, or extending the school day. Instead, these processes show you how to use your current time and resources in more targeted, effective ways. School staff should not work *harder*, but *collectively smarter*. Putting the ideas in this book into practice will help more students learn, and in turn, transition your faculty from seeing RTI as a *must* do to a *want* to!

Making a Case for Doing Things Differently

Professional learning communities recognize that until members of the organization "do" differently, there is no reason to anticipate different results.

—Richard DuFour, Rebecca DuFour, Robert Eaker, and
Thomas W. Many

A Story From Roosevelt Intermediate School

Roosevelt Intermediate School was considered a good school. Students seemed generally satisfied to habitually submit the work their teachers had assigned to them. Teachers were very content in their daily teaching routines, and students who came prepared with the necessary background knowledge seemed to navigate the school well. If a student wasn't successful in a class or the school, it was common for most teachers to suggest that he or she come in before or after school to get extra help.

Although no one said it outright, many whispered conversations took place in the hallways and faculty room about the reasons for lack of success at Roosevelt. One of the teachers seemed to sum up the general culture of the school, "I love my students, but some just choose not to learn. There are some students who have difficult home lives, while others just don't seem to get it after I teach a concept." With anxious frustration in her voice, she continued, "I'm working hard trying to deliver the massive number of standards required of me. If students don't grasp the concept during initial instruction, as much as I would like to, I just don't have the time to circle back around and help those who need it." The majority on staff shared this sentiment.

At the conclusion of each year, the leadership team and staff would meet to review results from Roosevelt's end-of-year summative assessments to gauge the progress of the school and student learning. The faculty emitted an audible sigh as the leadership team shared the results. As predicted, Roosevelt's results showed little growth. Teachers were frustrated. They worked hard delivering the overwhelming number of standards to students, but some just didn't get it. Likewise, the leadership team was equally frustrated because they had organized the teachers into loosely organized collaborative teams and had even spent precious school funds to send a few teachers to a recent PLC institute.

As the cloud of frustration consumed the meeting, a teacher sitting on the back row stood up. As the faculty quieted, the teacher spoke, "For twenty-two years, I have taught alongside you at Roosevelt Intermediate. Like you, I work hard each day. But this year, something is different for me. As we were reviewing the list of students who are not proficient on the end-of-year assessments, I recognized that my niece and nephew, whom I love dearly, were on that list. Her voice was shaking as she continued, "They are wonderful students, and like all of us, still learning. When I saw their names on the list of those who were not proficient, my heart sank. If they don't have the skills needed to be successful, I know from experience they are at risk of educational failure."

As the weight of this teacher's comments settled on the room, she concluded her thoughts with a single statement that seemed to shake the Roosevelt leadership and faculty to its cultural core. "I don't know how, but we *have* to do something different than we've done in the past. We can't keep losing these students."

As her profound words hung in the air, her fellow educators begin to nod as if to say, "Yes, we need to do things differently."

Roosevelt Intermediate School is like many schools across the United States. They are staffed with hardworking professionals who are committed to their students. Unfortunately, the pressure to teach the overwhelming number of standards during the short school year caused the staff at Roosevelt to establish a pattern of simply "covering" the standards. It's not that they weren't working hard; they just didn't know a better way. As a result, well-intentioned teachers defaulted to a frenzied delivery of standards with no time to assist those who might need extra help and support.

This chapter will make the case for *why* we need to do things differently in our schools and offer specific strategies and tools for *how* to get there.

Why We Need to Do Things Differently

To know what the right things are, we must first understand why we need change. According to the U.S. Department of Education's (2015) National Center for Education Statistics, the high school graduation rate in the United States increased to 81 percent for the 2012–2013 school year, the highest level since states adopted a new way of calculating graduation rates in 2013.

For educators, this is cause for celebration, as this was the fifth consecutive year for graduation rate increases. For this, we have reason to celebrate! But, let's not keep our party hats on too long. Keep in mind that 19 percent of youth didn't leave the system with a diploma or the skills needed to be successful in today's world. These are the students who, as research so painfully proves to us, will most likely struggle throughout their entire lives (Gewertz, 2019).

Further supporting the need for change, Stanford University professor emeritus Russell W. Rumberger's (2011) research on students who drop out of school validates this compelling case for ensuring students possess the skills they need to be successful:

> One of the most apparent and lasting impacts of dropping out is observed in the labor market. Dropouts are the least competitive workers in the job market because they have the least education. Even if they have skills and abilities, their lack of credential makes it more difficult for them to demonstrate those skills and abilities to a would-be employer. As a result, they are least likely to get a job, and the jobs they do get pay the lowest wages and do not offer benefits. (p. 88)

Success in today's world demands knowledge of critical course content and the 21st century skills of collaboration, creativity, problem solving, and critical thinking with an increasing need for digital and multicultural competencies. Without these skills and knowledge, students are woefully underprepared for today's world. As fellow educators, we understand the complexities of teaching a classroom of students with varied needs. Our collective responsibility as educators is to each and every student we serve. But we can't do it alone. It will take a collective, focused effort to ensure students acquire the skills and behaviors they need to be successful. The risk of losing students is too great.

Here's How

So what are the right things? Let's begin with foundational principles of effective practices that we will discuss in greater detail throughout this book. Strong, stable foundations are critical to the success of any organization. A building contractor would never consider building a house on a weak foundation. Without a solid foundation, any work will fail to stand. This same lesson holds true with effective intervention. The following foundational principles are an absolutely critical foundation for schools and teams to build on for success.

▽ Work in collaborative teaching teams.

▽ Implement effective Tier 1 teaching practices.

▽ Shift from a focus on teaching to learning.

▽ Establish a guaranteed and viable curriculum.

▽ Provide targeted common formative assessments.

▽ Identify obstacles to learning.

▽ Establish a flexible daily schedule.

Work in Collaborative Teaching Teams

There is not a single teacher, no matter how talented, who has all the skills needed to meet the diverse needs of every student he or she serves. If we are to ensure all students learn at high levels, it is essential that schools and teams utilize their collective expertise and experience to help all students. Teaching is no longer a labor in isolation but an exercise in teamwork. As teams work together in a collaborative manner (focusing their collective efforts on student learning), the effectiveness of the team increases. If schools are going to meet the varied, complex needs of every student they serve, teachers must work interdependently in collaborative teams (DuFour et al., 2016). Utilizing the collective expertise and talents of every member of the team, schools are better able to meet the needs of all students. Figure 1.1 details the work of effective teams.

Implement Effective Tier 1 Teaching Practices

A solid Tier 1 foundation, or initial teaching practices, is the essential step before we move on to effective Tier 2 interventions. Schools that may have weak or ineffective Tier 1 teaching practices will not solve their challenges by creating a system of Tier 2 supports. When this occurs, teachers and teams might rush through initial, critical Tier 1 instruction in order to place students in Tier 2 interventions with the expectation that the interventions will correct their learning. They won't. No intervention structure or support can compensate for poor Tier 1 teaching practices, which is why creating effective teacher teams is so important.

Shift From a Focus on Teaching to Learning

We believe this essential shift begins with asking the following simple question proposed in *Simplifying Response to Intervention: Four Essential Guiding Principles*: "Are we here to teach, or are we here to ensure that our students learn?" (Buffum et al., 2012, p. 17).

Answering the latter sounds simple enough, but a dramatic shift from an emphasis on teaching (and simply delivering massive amounts of content), to a laser-like focus on the critical elements of a curriculum that every student needs to learn to be successful requires a change in thinking and practice. Far too often, a focus on teaching occupies the majority of time in teacher conversations, trainings, and even educator evaluation legislation. Hattie (2012) reaffirms this frustration by stating, "I have almost reached the point at which I lose interest in discussion about teaching,

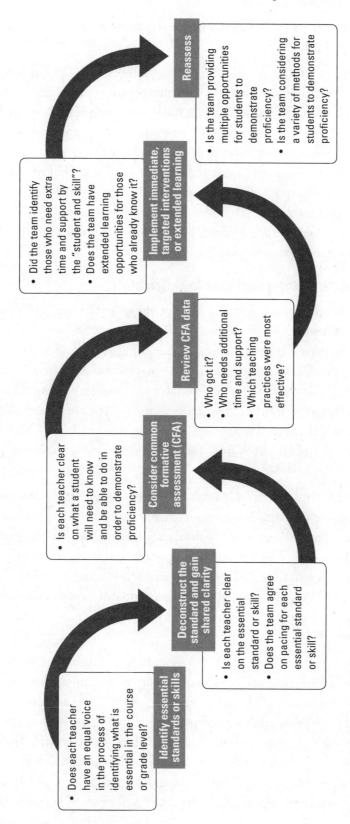

Reassess

- Is the team providing multiple opportunities for students to demonstrate proficiency?
- Is the team considering a variety of methods for students to demonstrate proficiency?

- Did the team identify those who need extra time and support by the "student and skill"?
- Does the team have extended learning opportunities for those who already know it?

Implement immediate, targeted interventions or extended learning

Review CFA data

- Who got it?
- Who needs additional time and support?
- Which teaching practices were most effective?

- Is each teacher clear on what a student will need to know and be able to do in order to demonstrate proficiency?

Consider common formative assessment (CFA)

Deconstruct the standard and gain shared clarity

- Is each teacher clear on the essential standard or skill?
- Does the team agree on pacing for each essential standard or skill?

- Does each teacher have an equal voice in the process of identifying what is essential in the course or grade level?

Identify essential standards or skills

Figure 1.1: The work of effective teams.

*Visit **go.SolutionTree.com/RTIatWork** for a free reproducible version of this figure.*

not because it is not important, but because it often prevents important discussions about learning" (p. 185).

As educational practitioners, we are in no way diminishing the importance of teaching. But in the end, if a teacher spends hours planning, preparing, and delivering a lesson and students don't learn, then he or she simply entertained students during this limited, valuable instructional time. To be more effective, our focus instead needs to be on *learning*, that is, examining how the results of our team's efforts impact student *learning*. Teams shouldn't discuss and plan to answer the question, "How can we push out all this curriculum in the limited time we have?" Instead, the question teams and school leaders should be asking is, "How can we maximize our time to ensure our students learn the essential skills they need to be successful in their course or grade level?"

Establish a Guaranteed and Viable Curriculum

As schools and teams focus on learning and the impact of instruction on learning, the question, "Learn what?" soon follows. Ask any educator, and you will hear the same response, "We have too many standards and not enough time to cover them." In order to cover a number of standards, educational researcher Robert J. Marzano states, "To cover all this content, you would have to change schooling from K–12 to K–22. . . . The sheer number of standards is the biggest impediment to implementing standards" (as cited in Scherer, 2001, p. 15). So the idea that all students will learn all the standards is impossible. There are just too many standards and too little time.

Whether referred to as *essential standards*, *essential learnings*, or *a guaranteed and viable curriculum*, the thinking is the same: teacher teams need to prioritize standards, coming to consensus on what is absolutely essential for students to know and be able to do as a result of the course or grade level. Trying to intervene with every student on every standard is impossible and will inevitably lead to a lack of specific intervention. Once teams identify those essential standards and skills, they must then engage in the work of breaking the standards into accessible, measurable learning targets.

Once teams identify what is essential in the standards and unpack those standards into measurable learning targets, common formative assessments become much more diagnostic and intervention much more targeted. Unless a team engages in the foundational work of establishing a guaranteed and viable curriculum, its assessments will become less targeted and interventions will begin to unravel. Thus, prior to developing a system of effective Tier 2 interventions, teams must first identify and come to consensus on what they will be assessing and intervening on. Make no mistake, this is the first critical step in developing an effective system of interventions.

Provide Targeted Common Formative Assessments

Following the creation of a guaranteed and viable curriculum, teams engage in building common formative assessments for three purposes: (1) to identify which students are proficient in the essential standard or skill; (2) to identify which students are in need of extra time and support; and (3) to engage teachers in professional conversations about which teaching practices elicit the best results.

Targeted common formative assessments focus on getting down to the student and skill level. While regular assessments can provide general learning feedback, *targeted common formative assessments* provide the teacher and learner with feedback that is targeted on the skill with which the student is proficient and identifies which skills or skills the student requires extra time and support to master.

Assessments should be more than just scores in the gradebook; teachers should use them to diagnostically help teams pinpoint areas in which individual students require additional Tier 2 time and support. Assessments then provide support using the team's collective strategy or the school's structure rather than each individual teacher simply providing support to his or her own students. Instead, teams demonstrate the collective thinking, "How do we best support *our* students?"

Identify Obstacles to Learning

Getting to targeted, effective interventions begins with first identifying what is preventing students from learning at high levels. Prior to providing an intervention, schools need to engage in the work of identifying the cause. Chapter 2 (page 29) will introduce a collective process for identifying the causes for a student's lack of success as well as designing interventions that address these causes.

Far too often, schools rush to build a system of interventions without a clear understanding of what they are intervening on. As a result, the interventions become less targeted and more generic. In order to provide targeted interventions, schools must identify the causes preventing students from learning at high levels, distinguish those causes the school has influence over, and then build an effective intervention structure that provides support for each cause.

Establish a Flexible Daily Schedule

As we examine the work of schools, we know teachers spend hours working to meet the needs of students. Today's educators work tirelessly planning, teaching, and assessing on behalf of their students. But what happens when, in spite of a teacher's best efforts, one or more students don't learn the concept or skill? Teachers feel a compelling urge to move forward. Yet, there are students who still need extra time and support to learn a concept or skill. From this comes the often-asked question,

"How can I find time to support students who need it with the extensive curriculum I need to deliver?" Coming in before and after school is no longer the answer. Effective Tier 2 intervention requires flexible time built into a school's daily schedule. Simply put, flexible time is time teachers build into the traditional school day that provides both teachers and students with extra time for learning.

Conclusion

The stories are compelling and the research is clear; we must continue to improve. The consequences of failure are too severe for our economy, our society, and our students. In order to accomplish this challenging moral imperative, schools, teams, and leaders must collectively think and work together, making substantive changes to schools, systems, and their approach to learning. Having been in education for a collective sixty years, we wholeheartedly concur with PLC at Work architect Richard DuFour's (2015) purposeful question each of us as educators should thoughtfully consider: "Will you act with a sense of urgency, as if the very lives of your students depend on your action, because in a very literal sense, more than at any other time in American history, they do?" (p. 254).

It comes down to this: not only *what* we do as educators, but *how* we do it dramatically impacts student lives, our economy, and our society. This journey is a process that starts with making the decision to do the following right things right.

▽ Think differently.

▽ Have different conversations.

▽ Rethink what happens in the classroom and within teams.

▽ Consider alternatives to our traditional time structures of school.

▽ Look at curriculum, instruction, and assessment through a more targeted lens.

Collectively, educators need to be creative, ingenious, and passionate. Oh, and by the way, your plans will not to be perfect the first time. You *will* make mistakes; this is part of the process. You will make decisions as a team or school that will seem fabulous at the time, but will struggle to get off the ground. Don't give up; this is a normal part of the process of learning together. The important thing to remember is to keep thinking, continue discussing, and most importantly, persist in being creative. Immerse yourself into a true learning community with your colleagues. As renowned author Malcolm Gladwell (2002) states, "If you want to bring a fundamental change in people's belief and behavior . . . you need to create a community around them, where those new beliefs can be practiced and expressed and nurtured" (p. 173).

As your teams and school continue to think, practice, and experiment, your efforts will be rewarded.

Let's examine the existing practices in schools and teams to determine if they are truly effective. Let's carefully look at daily teaching strategies to see if we are merely delivering content or ensuring students learn. Let's explore our existing schedules, structures, and practices and ensure we are providing effective Tier 2 learning time for all students. Finally, let's join together and make deep, meaningful changes to learning that will impact students and our society. The hour has come. The time is now. Effort will not be enough. We need to make sure, amid the demands of day-to-day school, that we are doing the *right* work right; that we are truly engaged in those things that ensure all students learn at high levels. Otherwise, even our most valiant efforts will be lost. You can do this. We can do this. It's time.

The "Chapter 1: Key Considerations Rubric" reproducibles on pages 27–28 serve as a touchstone for schools and teams to evaluate their current reality and inspire conversations regarding areas of strength for the team or school, areas to focus on, and next steps. Teams can use this simple rubric during team meetings or with the whole faculty as a way to foster discussions about implementing effective RTI in their school.

Big Ideas for Chapter 1

The following six big ideas provide an overview of the most important concepts from this chapter.

1. Teachers must work in meaningful collaborative teaching teams utilizing the strengths of each team member.

2. The most effective intervention is to implement effective Tier 1 teaching practices.

3. Teams need to focus on what students learn rather than what they teach.

4. Teams must engage in the work of giving curricular priority to those standards deemed as essential for students to know and be able to do.

5. Teams should use common formative assessments to identify the targeted needs of each student.

6. Schools need to build flexible time into their daily schedules to provide extra learning time for teachers and students.

Chapter 1: Key Considerations Rubric

Directions: With your school or team, read the key considerations listed in the far-left column of the rubric. Evaluate where your team or school currently is and what steps you need to establish in your daily practice to achieve these goals. Once completed, with your team discuss your areas of strength, areas of challenge, and next steps for your school or team.

Embedded

This is how we do business. We do this without thinking about it; it's just part of our school or team culture.

Developing

We get it and do fairly well in implementing this into our daily work.

Limited

We have some individuals in our school or team who understand and implement this, but it's sporadic at best.

No Evidence

There is little to no evidence of this; we have work to do!

Key Considerations	Embedded	Developing	Limited	No Evidence
We fundamentally believe *all* students can and will learn in our school.				
Our school schedule provides adequate time for students who require additional support.				
The focus of our school is to ensure students will learn essential elements within the curriculum.				

page 1 of 2

An area of **strength** for us:

A **challenging** area for us:

Our **next steps**:

page 2 of 2

Using Collaborative Teams for Effective Intervention

A boat doesn't go forward if each one is rowing their own way.

—Swahili proverb

A Story From Sunnyside Middle School

The teachers at Sunnyside Middle School are committed, hardworking professionals who want the very best for their students. They come in early each day ready to help their students learn. Principal Jennings energetically announced to the faculty that they were going to work to ensure every student learns at high levels, and they were going to become a professional learning community. Principal Jennings and the leadership team at Sunnyside led the staff in reviewing research on what happens to students who leave school without the skills needed to be successful. The leadership team then facilitated the staff in a deep dive into the learning data at their school. As the staff reviewed the learning data, they were reminded that they already knew there were many students leaving their school without the skills needed to be successful. Most of the staff were convinced they needed to do things differently than in the past. Principal Jennings's enthusiasm about this new idea of ensuring every student learns at high levels was inspiring; however, reality set in as they reviewed the current school interventions.

The first of their school's interventions was simple. If students needed additional help, they could come in before or after school to receive assistance. The thinking was that any student who needed extra assistance would choose to come in to receive it. As the staff reviewed the effectiveness of this intervention, they came to the harsh, yet predictable realization that it was ineffective in helping them accomplish their new purpose. The only students staff were seeing before and after school were those who needed to raise their A– to an A; in other words, those who were already academically successful. These were certainly not the students the staff was hoping or needing to see. As the staff explored further, they realized 80 percent of their students rode the bus to and from school, and unless the student could convince his or her parents, grandparents, or some other guardian to miss work and bring the student to school, it was virtually impossible for him or her to receive help. Further complicating this strategy was that the majority of students were involved in activities before or after school (for example, tending to siblings or participating in extracurricular activities and clubs). As the staff evaluated this intervention, it became painfully clear this strategy was seemingly ineffective.

The only other intervention the school provided for students was a study hall, which the school had cleverly named Learning Enhancement (as if a simple name change would change the ambiguous nature of a traditional study hall). Teachers placed students in Learning Enhancement based on one indicator— they were failing a class. It didn't matter why they were failing; they were all simply failing. The students placed in the Learning Enhancement were all failing, but as the staff soon discovered, they were failing for a variety of reasons.

Some students just needed a little extra time and support to become proficient in a particular concept or skill. Some students simply refused to do the required work. There were even a few students placed in Learning Enhancement because they were too disorganized to function successfully in class. The school assigned Learning Enhancement to a teacher who needed a couple of extra periods to have a full schedule and told the teacher to "catch them up"! Rather than providing targeted intervention, this teacher dutifully hustled around the Learning Enhancement classroom, helping as many as possible, while simply trying to survive the chaotic class period.

As the staff of Sunnyside discovered, students were failing for a variety of reasons but were all provided with the same generic intervention. They quickly realized that neither of the interventions provided by the school were effective and soon after, a sense of urgency set in; they needed to do things differently.

Upon returning to the classroom, reality set in for the teachers at Sunnyside. The complexities of their compelling purpose of ensuring every student learns at high levels seemed like a great idea, but as they reviewed their current school interventions, this new purpose overwhelmed the teachers. On top of this, there was a mountain of standards they needed to teach before the end of the year. Although the staff understood why they needed to ensure every student learns at high levels, the reality of how this would happen seemed simply overwhelming. Overall, there was a sense of confusion regarding this new vision, where to start, and what work would be involved in helping achieve this purpose. As compelling and passionate as this new purpose was, the staff was unclear as to even where to begin.

Like many schools, the staff at Sunnyside Middle School are attempting to provide Tier 2 support through opportunities to learn and by grouping students with varied needs into one learning enhancement class. At Sunnyside, if students require extra assistance, teachers simply encourage them to come in outside of normal school hours. Coupled with this is the fact that the few interventions that Sunnyside provides are not targeted on specific skills with which students are deficient. Instead, the hardworking staff at Sunnyside rely on a generic learning enhancement class to improve their grade to passing.

Complicating things further, the staff feels immense pressure to simply get the overwhelming volume of standards delivered to their students. Teachers don't target interventions on students' needs or try to build flexible time into the school day to re-teach concepts. Like many schools, Sunnyside's honorable efforts at providing Tier 2 support are frustrating.

This chapter will explain *why* we need to do things differently and offer specific strategies and tools for *how* to get there.

Why We Need to Do Things Differently

There is little debate regarding the effectiveness of a team approach to student learning. Effective schools utilize the talents and strengths of all people in the school to ensure every student learns at high levels. With the varied and complex needs of students, it is virtually impossible for a single educator to think he or she possesses all of the skills, experience, and talents to accomplish that goal. This is the crossroad most school staffs will inevitably face, asking themselves the following questions.

▽ "Do we allow hardworking teachers to simply close their doors and deliver curriculum over the course of the year knowing that some students will miss critical content?"

▽ "Do we begin to organize our schools into hardworking teams driven by a single purpose: ensuring all students learn essential content?"

As schools move from being simply the deliverers of curriculum to organizing themselves into a PLC driven by powerful teams with laser-like focus on ensuring every student in the school learns at high levels, their work becomes a much more strategic, coordinated effort. As schools transition their thinking, behaviors, and practices from *me* to *we* and from *you* to *us*, all students stand to benefit from these combined, collective efforts in the school's coordinated response.

Three Essential Teams

At the foundation of a school's effective intervention structure are three essential teams. Each of these teams must be present in a school in order to provide the targeted approach needed to implement an effective intervention system. Each team performs fundamental tasks essential to a successful intervention structure.

Teacher Teams

Teacher teams are at the heart of a PLC and key to an effective intervention system. According to DuFour et al. (2006), a teacher team is made up of "a group of people working *interdependently* to achieve a common goal, for which members are held *mutually accountable*" (p. 40).

As outlined by PLC experts and authors DuFour et al. (2016), the four critical questions of a PLC drive the collective work of teacher teams:

1. What do students need to know and be able to do?
2. How will we know when they have learned it?
3. How will we respond if they haven't learned it?
4. How will we extend the learning of those who already know it? (p. 251)

Teacher teams have specific, primary responsibilities in the development of an effective intervention structure that supports the targeted learning of all students. Teacher teams lead these responsibilities and contribute to the overall effectiveness of a school's intervention structure. These specific responsibilities include the following.

▽ **Identify essential learning outcomes:** Teacher teams must clearly identify the essential student learning outcomes for each unit of instruction in each course. Once identified, teams then must deconstruct the essentials into measurable learning targets. Consensus and clarity on these essential learning outcomes provide a common understanding and consistency from class to class and from teacher to teacher.

▽ **Provide effective Tier 1 instruction and determine the effect on student learning:** Teacher teams are responsible for providing effective initial instruction. They should be cautious not to rush through their initial Tier 1 instruction in an attempt to move students to Tier 2 intervention. A good rule of thumb is that generally three of every four students should "get it" if the initial instruction is sound. If, for example, only half the students in the class understand the concept after initial instruction, a teacher should not refer the half of the class who didn't "get it" to intervention. This is not an intervention problem; instead, teams should examine the initial instruction. Again, a primary responsibility of teacher teams is to provide quality Tier 1 instruction.

▽ **Commonly assess student learning:** Once initial instruction is complete, teacher teams utilize common formative assessments. Each teacher gives an assessment with team agreement on what constitutes proficiency. After administering the common formative assessment, teams use the results to determine the following.

  ▶ Which students are proficient in the essential outcome or learning target

  ▶ Which students require extra time and support in order to achieve proficiency

  ▶ Which teaching practices elicited the best results

These common assessment results are the central focus of a team's collaborative meetings and serve to assist teams in providing targeted Tier 2 intervention.

▽ **Identify students in need of intervention about every three weeks:** With each unit of instruction approximately three weeks in length, teams should identify students in need of Tier 2 intervention approximately every three weeks based on the targeted area, as identified through the common formative assessment.

▽ **Take primary responsibility for Tier 2 academic interventions:** Teacher teams take the lead in providing extra time and support for students who need it. Teams decide which member of the team will intervene on which essential outcome or target. Who better to provide quality Tier 2 intervention than the teacher on the team who taught the concept the best?

Leadership Team

Another team critical to an effective intervention structure is the school's leadership team. The school leadership typically consists of the school administration, department or team leaders, and others of influence within the school. Simply put, the school's leadership team is responsible for building consensus about the school's mission of collective responsibility for student learning. The leadership team creates structures and supports in the school that ensure students who require extra time and support to learn at high levels receive them. The leadership team works to provide a school culture and daily climate focused on high levels of learning for all students, instilling the belief that *all* students in the school will learn. As the teacher team takes primary responsibility for Tier 2 academic interventions, the school leadership team takes responsibility for supplemental supports in motivation, behavior, and attendance.

Intervention Team

The third critical team necessary for an effective school intervention structure is the intervention team. The school intervention team coordinates all available resources to support students who need intervention. These resources may include counselors, psychologists, speech and language pathologists, subject specialists, instructional aides, and any other person who can assist a student with learning. The coordination of these resources assists a school in providing immediate, targeted intervention.

Ensuring every student in a school learns at high levels is a tall order for any school. As schools work to accomplish this task, they first need to get clarity on what is preventing their students from learning at high levels. Gaining collective clarity on these things allows the school to develop interventions targeted on student needs.

Three Tiers of RTI

As mentioned earlier, we can separate a school's response for students needing extra time and support into three distinct tiers that work to provide support for teachers and students alike. Teams can work together to make sure these teachers deliver these tiers of instruction and intervention effectively.

Tier 1: Core Instruction

Tier 1 represents the necessary elements of a highly effective core instructional program that serves as a foundation for the school, staff, and students. Tier 1 clearly provides the expectations for all students. Included in Tier 1 are the elements of effective initial instruction. Let's be clear, no intervention structure or support will compensate for ineffective initial instruction; it's that simple. Schools and teams need to spend time understanding what effective Tier 1 instruction looks like (outlined in greater detail in chapters 3–5). Unless schools and teams understand and implement effective Tier 1 practices as part of their initial instruction, Tier 2 conversations will be misguided and unproductive.

Clarity at Tier 1 is essential if schools and teams are to provide effective Tier 2 supplementary supports. This is reaffirmed in *Pyramid Response to Intervention: RTI, Professional Learning Communities, and How to Respond When Kids Don't Learn* (Buffum et al., 2009), which notes, "*Core program*, also commonly referred to as *Tier 1*, *base*, *primary*, or *universal* program, refers to a school's initial instructional practices—in other words, the teaching and school experiences that all kids receive every day" (p. 74). For the purposes of this book, we will refer to these practices as *Tier 1* (revisit figure I.1, page 4, and figure I.6, page 8).

Tier 2: Supplemental Interventions

Tier 2 interventions, or *supplemental interventions*, are designed to provide targeted assistance for students who need extra time and support in meeting the Tier 1 expectations. Simply put, Tier 2 interventions are supports for students *so they don't fall behind* the pace of their peers. Most students, if not all, at some time during their learning will require extra time and support to meet proficiency in an essential standard. Tier 2 interventions provide time and support during the school day to assist these students in meeting those schoolwide Tier 1 expectations.

In an effort to provide interventions, well-intentioned schools will often build a series of interventions with little regard to the specific needs of each student. It is critical that prior to developing interventions, schools engage in the work of identifying *what* is preventing their students from learning at high levels. Schools need to have great clarity regarding those obstacles. Prior to developing a system of interventions, an essential step for leadership teams and staff is to engage in conversations and the accompanying work about those things that prevent students in their schools from learning at high levels.

Tier 3: Intensive Remediation

The focus of Tier 3 is to provide intense remediation strategies to help students who are significantly behind their grade-level peers. Often referred to as *closing the gap*, Tier 3 remediation focuses on decreasing the level in which the student is behind. While Tier 2 intervention is designed to keep students from *falling behind* their peers, Tier 3 remediation is designed to help students *catch up to* their peers. Tier 2 intervention focuses on targeted students who need a little extra time and support to grasp a concept, whereas Tier 3 remediation focuses on individual students who require intense support to catch up to grade level.

Here's How

Building Tier 2 interventions that provide the necessary time and support for students can seem like an overwhelming task. Initially, staff may attempt to replicate school with successful interventions. However, instead of simply replicating another school's interventions, the leadership team should discuss with the staff what is preventing students from learning at high levels and the critical importance of using the collective strengths of each teacher to ensure every student receives targeted time and support.

Once schools can identify the purpose for a student's lack of success, they can design interventions that target the need instead of providing broad, nontargeted interventions. Instead of a single teacher being responsible for ensuring all of his or her students learn, a team and school assume this shared responsibility. This is what we refer to as moving from "These students are mine" thinking to "We as a staff are going to use our collective strengths to ensure that all students in our school learn at high levels. They are *ours*!"

Simply put, schools must do the following.

▽ Gain clarity on what is preventing students from learning

▽ Move from *mine* to *ours*

Gain Clarity on What Is Preventing Students From Learning

Schools sometimes develop interventions without real clarity as to the causes for a student's struggle in school. Schools should first identify the causes for a student's struggle. The school principal, team leader, or designated facilitator can lead this collaborative work in identifying areas that are preventing students from learning at high levels, identifying deficiencies in their current intervention structure, and developing interventions based on students' identified needs.

Teams can begin this process by taking the seven following steps.

1. Place teachers in teams at tables and provide them with sticky notes and pens or pencils.

2. On sheets of poster paper, write the following headings and post them on the walls around the room:

   ▸ Academics

   ▸ Behaviors

   ▸ Other

3. Ask each team to discuss the following question, "What is preventing our students from learning at high levels?"

4. Have each team write its thoughts—one thought for each sticky note—and place the notes on the poster paper that best represents the thought (academics, behavior, or other).

5. Once all teams complete this task, the principal, leadership team, and staff discuss those things over which the school has little to no control (for example, unsupportive parents or a student's home environment). Set those notes aside.

6. With the remaining notes, ask the question, "Does our school have an effective intervention or support system in place to assist students with this deficit?"

7. For those areas for which the school doesn't have an intervention, the principal or leadership team engages the staff in conversations about what structure the school can adjust, modify, or create in order to provide the necessary support for students in these targeted areas.

Keep in mind that this is not a task to complete but a process; it is a process that won't be concluded in a single meeting. This ongoing process is designed to engage staff in thinking about *what* is preventing students from learning at high levels and then in designing targeted interventions that address each area.

Move From *Mine* to *Ours*

Let's be honest, the task of ensuring every student learns at high levels can seem overwhelming. Students come to the classroom with a variety of abilities and challenges. The idea that one teacher will have all of the abilities, talents, and skills needed to meet the varied needs of every student is impossible. We have had the opportunity to work with schools and districts around the world. During this time, we have met some unbelievably talented, experienced teachers who possess skills second to none in education. But of all the wonderful teachers and leaders we have met, we have yet to meet one who possesses all the skills and abilities needed to meet the varied needs of every student. As such, it is then incumbent on schools to organize highly effective collaborative teams focused on a common goal. These teams "work together *interdependently* to achieve a *common goal* for which members are held *mutually accountable*" (DuFour, DuFour, Eaker, & Many, 2006, p. 26), utilizing the collective strengths of each team member (and school) to move schools closer to accomplishing their compelling purpose.

Along with this is a necessary paradigm shift. Rather than seeing students as *yours* or *mine*, effective teams view students as *ours*. Conversations surrounding the learning of *my students* will quickly be replaced with targeted conversations about how the team can utilize their collective expertise and strengths to make sure that *our students* learn. The research is clear and compelling regarding the practice of working in effective teams to ensure every student learns at high levels. Educational consultants Kathleen Fulton and Ted Britton (2011) reaffirm this team approach to student learning:

> We now have compelling evidence that when teachers team up with their colleagues they are able to create a culture of success in schools, leading to teaching improvements and student learning gains. The clear policy and practice implication is that great teaching is a team sport. (p. 4)

In *Professional Capital: Transforming Teaching in Every School*, educational researchers Andy Hargreaves and Michael Fullan (2012) speak concisely about the critical nature of teachers working in collaborative teams to ensure every student learns at high levels:

> *Teaching like a pro* means planning, teaching, improving teaching, and often doing teaching as not an isolated individual but as part of a high-performing team. . . . All successful organizations in all walks of life . . . build effective teams as a core part of performance. (p. 22)

We concur with the research and further reiterate the critical step of schools organizing themselves into effective teams. Schools that attempt to provide intervention without first organizing themselves into collaborative teams focused on the work of learning together limit the effectiveness of their efforts.

Schools can organize teachers into a variety of teams in order to accomplish their purpose. Large or small, schools can organize teams that utilize the strengths of each teacher. How schools organize teams is less important than what the teams focus on: *student learning.*

Gaining clarity on the right work of teams is an essential step in the intervention process. "Clarity precedes competence" (Schmoker, 2004, p. 85), and no truer words can apply to the work of teams as they build a foundation for effective intervention. In a hurry to develop a system of interventions, some school teams might fail to spend the necessary time with PLC critical questions 1 and 2 (see page 9). More often than not, schools address these questions by simply identifying a few essential standards and then developing a loose, untargeted assessment they quickly label a common assessment. Take it from experience, teams must spend the necessary time to get clarity on the answers to PLC critical questions 1 and 2 to create the foundation needed for effective, targeted intervention. Consider the following questions that teams must address to gain clarity in addressing PLC critical questions 1 and 2.

1. What do students need to know and be able to do?

   ▸ Has our team identified and come to consensus on the skills absolutely critical for all students to know and be able to do?

   ▸ Has our team deconstructed these essential standards into measurable learning targets?

   ▸ Does our team have agreed-on clarity regarding what a proficient student will know and be able to do regarding each essential standard?

2. How will we know when they have learned it?

   ▸ Has our team developed or identified a way to collectively assess student learning on each essential standard or target?

▸ Is our team able to identify students who require extra time and support on the essential standard or target level? Down to the student and skill?

Unless teams have a deep level of understanding when addressing PLC critical questions 1 and 2, their intervention efforts will lack the targeted effort needed to be truly effective. To have effective Tier 2 interventions, teams must spend the necessary time getting clear about the essential standards and targets on which they will intervene, and how they will know if a student requires extra time and support. Teams can only accomplish this through collaborative work around the standards and assessments.

Conclusion

As stated earlier, clarity is critical to effective intervention and support. Many well-intentioned teams and schools immediately build an intervention strategy and schedule without first gaining clarity on what is actually causing students to struggle and what specifically they will intervene on. The result is often confusing Tier 2 interventions that leave teachers unclear on what students should do. Teams spend time discussing what each teacher will do during these interventions instead of each student's learning needs.

The "Chapter 2: Key Considerations Rubric" reproducibles on pages 41–42 serve as a touchstone for schools and teams to evaluate their current reality and inspire conversations regarding areas of strength for the team or school, areas to focus on, and next steps. Teams can use this simple rubric during team meetings or with the whole faculty as a way to foster discussions about implementing effective RTI in their school.

Big Ideas for Chapter 2

The following seven big ideas provide an overview of the most important concepts from this chapter.

1. Effective intervention structures are built on a three-tier system.

2. Schools developing an effective intervention structure need to have three essential teams: teacher teams, a leadership team, and an intervention team.

3. Schools and teams must utilize their collective strengths to move closer to accomplishing the purpose of ensuring every student learns at high levels.

4. Teams need to shift from seeing students as *yours* and *mine* to *ours*.

5. No interventions will compensate for ineffective Tier 1 instruction.

6. Teams must have collective clarity in answering PLC critical questions 1 and 2 prior to developing effective Tier 2 interventions.

7. Schools and teams must have collective clarity on *what* the causes are for students not learning at high levels so they can modify or develop effective interventions and supports to address these deficiencies.

Chapter 2: Key Considerations Rubric

Directions: With your school or team, read the key considerations listed in the far-left column of the rubric. Evaluate where your team or school currently is and what steps you need to establish in your daily practice to achieve these goals. Once completed, with your team discuss your areas of strength, areas of challenge, and next steps for your school or team.

Embedded

This is how we do business. We do this without thinking about it; it's just part of our school or team culture.

Developing

We get it and do fairly well in implementing this into our daily work.

Limited

We have some individuals in our school or team who understand and implement this, but it's sporadic at best.

No Evidence

There is little to no evidence of this; we have work to do!

Key Considerations	Embedded	Developing	Limited	No Evidence
We are organized into collaborative teams that utilize the collective strengths of each team member to ensure our students learn.				
We view students as *our* students and not *mine* and *yours*.				
As a school, we are clear on the specific causes that prevent our students from learning at high levels and address only those within our influence or control.				

page 1 of 2

Key Considerations	Embedded	Developing	Limited	No Evidence
Our teams have collective clarity regarding PLC critical questions 1 and 2: 1. What do students need to know and be able to do? 2. How will we know when they have learned it?				

An area of **strength** for us:

An area of **challenge** for us:

Our **next steps**:

Getting to Targeted and Specific Interventions

It doesn't really matter how fast you're going if you're heading in the wrong direction.

—Stephen R. Covey

A Story From Madison Middle School

In preparation for a workshop at Madison Middle School, Sharon Kramer schedules a conference call to determine the specific objectives for the day. As she listens to the principal and teacher leaders, it is clear they want to focus on support for students who demonstrate a need for more time to learn the curriculum. Sharon asks the following clarifying questions.

- "Are there common expectations for curriculum and learning mapped out for the school year?"
- "Are teachers at the same grade level and in the same content area teaching the same units at the same time?"
- "Are students learning the most important essential learnings, and do these learnings align with state standards?"
- "Are collaborative teams spending time prioritizing and deconstructing the state standards into manageable learning targets?"
- "Do teams have a shared understanding of what the standards mean and, more important, what it would look like if a student could actually do them well?"
- "Are students engaged in understanding and articulating the learning targets?"

The responses to these questions were an astonishing *no*! The school leaders' responses included the following remarks.

- "We do not have a focus on the priority or power state standards. They are all important."
- "We are teaching units, but each teacher decides what unit to teach, the content of the unit, and when to teach it."
- "Most of the staff believe this is an individual decision because each teacher has a different teaching style and philosophy. We could never be on the same pacing or unit."
- "We understand the standards individually, but we rarely discuss them as a team."

It was clear Madison did not have certain access for all students to additional time and support. In addition, it would be impossible to provide the targeted and specific supports to help all students without a clear understanding of what students need to know and be able to do. In other words, until the school establishes common learning expectations, it would be impossible to intervene since the staff do not know what the targets of instruction or Tier 2 interventions might be.

This scenario plays out all too often in many schools. When a school answers these questions concerning curriculum in this random manner, then it is obvious that it does not embrace a common curriculum, pacing, and opportunities to learn.

This chapter will explain *why* we need to do things differently when getting to targeted and specific interventions and offer specific strategies and tools for *how* to get there.

Why We Need to Do Things Differently

Getting to targeted and specific interventions that ensure student learning begins with collaborative teams building shared knowledge about what students need to learn, determining what proficiency looks like, and deciding how students will demonstrate their learning. This is the work of teams in recurring cycles on a unit-by-unit basis. Figure 3.1 shows the learning-assessment-intervention cycle.

In the learning-assessment-intervention cycle, teams collaboratively plan each unit to ensure common expectations for learning in every classroom. The emphasis is on the collective thinking and shared knowledge, not necessarily the format of the unit plan. The purpose of the unit plan is to design clear and cohesive instruction, assessments, and interventions that ensure student learning.

Implementing Tier 2 interventions effectively depends on many factors, most importantly, planning instruction around what students should know and be able to do and establishing a guaranteed and viable curriculum.

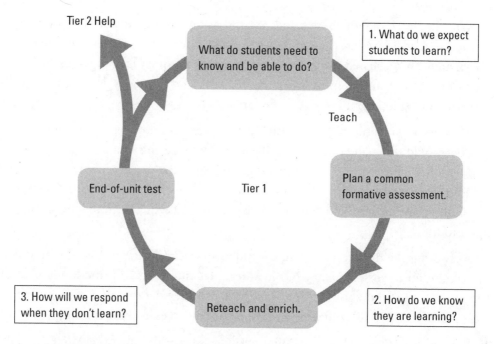

Source: *Adapted from Buffum & Mattos, 2015, p. 17.*

Figure 3.1: Learning-assessment-intervention cycle.

What Students Need to Know and Be Able to Do

We often meet with collaborative teacher teams as they plan instruction and interventions. As mentioned previously, most often instructional planning focuses on answering the four PLC critical questions (DuFour et al., 2016):

1. What do students need to know and be able to do?

2. How will we know when they have learned it?

3. How will we respond if they haven't learned it?

4. How will we extend the learning of those who already know it? (p. 251)

Hattie (2009) says:

> Teachers need to know the learning intentions and success criteria of their lessons, know how well they are attaining these criteria, and know where to go next in light of the criteria of: "Where are you going?", "How are you going?" and "Where to next?" (p. 239)

As teams begin to plan a unit of instruction, they answer each of these questions. Teachers sometimes gloss over question 1 and often don't even discuss it. When we ask teams how they answer the first question, they typically respond, "Oh don't worry we have state standards, Common Core standards, district pacing guides, and textbooks that align to one of these documents."

When we pick one of these standards and ask team members to quickly write what the standard means, there are often several versions of what it exactly entails. It is apparent that a shared team understanding of the standards does not exist. Each individual teacher makes meaning of the standards and translates that meaning into classroom instruction.

More important, the responses usually vary even more if we pose this question, "What would this standard look like if the students did this at a proficient or even higher level?" This is the question that digs deep into defining proficiency and rigor. Without agreement on this response, it is difficult for teams to plan instruction, administer assessments, and determine when a student requires more time and support to learn.

Answering the question, "What do students need to know and be able to do?" is paramount to answering any of the other three questions. If teams are not clear about *what* students should learn, then how will they determine if students have learned or how to intervene when they don't or how to extend the learning?

PLC critical question 1 is the foundation for answering the other three critical questions. Teams cannot get to targeted and specific interventions without deeply understanding what they are teaching and being able to clearly articulate what proficiency or evidence of learning is acceptable.

A Guaranteed and Viable Curriculum

"There's too much to teach!" This is often the outcry of teachers everywhere. So many standards, so little time! We agree. And not all standards are created equal. Some standards actually are absolutely *essential to know* and others are *nice to know*. Marzano (2003) suggests that a guaranteed and viable curriculum based on a clear list of priority standards or essential outcomes is the number-one opportunity to raise the level of student achievement. The *guaranteed curriculum* refers to the opportunity to learn. In other words, teams should define *what* they will guarantee all students will learn when they leave their grade or course. *Viable* refers to the opportunity to learn deeply, not just cover content. This means the teacher can address the content standards adequately during the allotted instructional time.

Determining a guaranteed and viable curriculum requires teams to clearly understand the standards teachers are expected to teach with enough time to teach them deeply. In most cases, teachers feel compelled to teach all the standards at each grade level or in every course, plus review everything students may have forgotten. Given the number of standards and the length of the school year, this is virtually impossible.

In addition, pacing of the curriculum requires teachers to teach so quickly that not much is really taught to mastery. An example involves teaching English parts of speech. When we talk with teachers at the ninth-grade level and ask them if they teach parts of speech, they typically respond, "Students have no concept of how to use parts of speech, so we need to teach them." If we ask middle school teachers the same question, they usually respond in the same way, adding, "Parts of speech are so important in high school that we spend an entire unit on them." Finally, if we ask elementary teachers if they teach parts of speech, they usually respond by saying, "Oh yes, it is really a skill students need in middle school," and kindergarten teachers join in by saying, "We teach nouns and verbs!" It appears that we are all teaching parts of speech but nowhere are we expecting students to master that skill. Determining the guaranteed curriculum means each grade-level teacher clearly understands what he or she owns and will teach to mastery. The problem is that no one can teach all the standards and ensure students actually master them in the allotted time. There's too much to teach!

Author, adolescent literacy expert, and high school teacher Kelly Gallagher (2009) states, "When teachers try to cram twenty-two years of curriculum into a K–12 time frame, everyone loses. . . . Students develop into memorizers instead of into thinkers" (p. 11).

A review of the standards indicates there are fewer standards now than, for example, in 2010. In the United States, most states are reducing the number of standards and increasing the rigor. This does not mean we no longer need to determine the most important or priority standards; increased rigor typically means more instructional time will be necessary to teach the concepts deeply. For example, a careful examination of the Common Core State Standards reveals that although the standards have been reduced, there is still too much to teach (see table 3.1).

Table 3.1: Number of Common Core Standards for English Language Arts 6–12

Grade Level	Literature	Informational Text	Foundational Skills	Writing	Speaking Listening	Language	Total
6	9	10	n/a	28	10	21	78
7	9	10	n/a	28	10	19	76
8	9	10	n/a	28	10	21	78
9–10	9	10	n/a	28	10	18	75
11–12	9	10	n/a	28	10	17	74

Source: Ainsworth, 2010.
Source for standards: NGA & CCSSO, 2010a.

Common Core mathematics standards are actually fewer in number, but with the increased levels of rigor, there is still too much to teach:

> The issue of whether or not to prioritize the standards . . . should never be reduced simply to a "numbers" game, especially when fewer standards may contain increased rigor that will require more instructional time and learning opportunities for students to fully grasp them. (Ainsworth, 2010, pp. 52–53)

See table 3.2.

Table 3.2: Number of Common Core Mathematics Standards Grades 6–8

Grade Level	Ratio and Proportions	Number Systems	Expressions and Equations	Geometry	Statistics	Probability Functions	Total
6	7	15	12	4	9	n/a	47
7	7	11	6	6	13	n/a	43
8	n/a	2	13	12	4	5	36

Source: Ainsworth, 2010.
Source for standards: NGA & CCSSO, 2010b.

When everything is important, nothing is really important. Teachers often race to cover the curriculum. Gallagher (2009) indicates that sprinting to cover the curriculum sacrifices deep, rich teaching and chips away at student motivation and curiosity.

From our experience, teachers often complain about the sheer amount of curriculum. Lack of time to teach is usually their number-one complaint. When teachers try to cover the entire list of standards, it greatly decreases the opportunities for the practice, feedback, and repetition students need to own their learning. Also, when teachers attempt to assess all the standards, the classroom becomes a testing factory. This reminder from University of California, Los Angeles professor emeritus W. James Popham (2003) rings true:

> It is critical that all of the assessed standards be truly significant. From an instructional perspective, it is better for tests to measure a handful of powerful skills accurately than it is for tests to do an inaccurate job of measuring many skills. (p. 143)

How can we determine the most important common learning expectations to ensure a guaranteed and viable curriculum?

Here's How

A guaranteed and viable curriculum is intended to focus each grade level and course on the most important standards, the must knows. It requires a deep understanding of the meaning of each standard and exactly what students are expected to know and be able to do to demonstrate proficiency. Common learning expectations begin with determining these essential standards. For example, biology must be the same course regardless of which teacher teaches it. The following three steps ensure a common curriculum and a shared understanding of the essential knowledge, skills, and concepts that teachers will teach and all students will learn.

1. Identify essential standards.

2. Deconstruct or unwrap essential standards to identify embedded learning targets.

3. Track learning progressions for targeted interventions.

Teams may reverse the first two steps in this process. When the standards are unfamiliar to teachers, it may be better to deconstruct (or unwrap) the standards first to gain clarity about their meaning before determining the essential (or priority) standards. As teachers deconstruct or unwrap standards, they also identify learning targets that support the standards. If the deconstruction process occurs first, teachers should still prioritize standards, not individual learning targets.

Identify Essential Standards

Essential standards are the carefully selected subset of the total list of grade- and course-specific standards in each content area that teachers guarantee all students must know and be able to do by the end of each school year to be prepared to enter the next grade level or course. Teachers develop common formative assessments on these standards. Students who have not mastered standards receive more time and support. Those who have mastered the standards receive extensions. While these priorities do not represent the entire curriculum, it is the content the team will ensure *every* student masters. This process is about prioritization, not elimination. Standards, assessment, curriculum, and instruction expert and consultant Larry Ainsworth (2013) states:

> Left to their own professional *opinions* when faced with the task of narrowing a voluminous number of student learning outcomes, educators naturally "pick and choose" those they know and like best, the ones for which they have materials and lessons plans or activities, and those most likely to appear on state tests. (p. 16)

Given all the standards in every grade and content area, how do we decide what is most important for students to know and be able to do? According to educator and leadership expert Douglas Reeves (2002), the most efficient process for determining which standards are essential or priority standards, is to apply the following three criteria: (1) endurance, (2) leverage, and (3) readiness.

1. **Endurance:** Knowledge and skills of value beyond a single test date. Will the standards be employed exactly as they are in life beyond the school walls? Do they represent how things are really done?

2. **Leverage:** Knowledge and skills of value in multiple disciplines. Is the standard transferrable and even necessary for learners to access skills and content in other areas or fields?

3. **Readiness:** Knowledge and skills necessary for success at the next level of instruction or grade level or on a state test. Is the standard a building block on which other standards are contingent?

When considering whether to select one similar standard over another, determine which one is the more comprehensive or rigorous over the one that is more foundational. Keep in mind that in addition to endurance, leverage, and readiness, essential standards are what teachers will spend the majority of their instructional time teaching, assessing, discussing, and intervening on or extending.

Teachers can determine essential standards in several ways. In some instances, district teams composed of representatives from several schools convene, select the essential standards, and share their work with teachers to gather feedback. Districts may also ask teams from each school to submit their selected essential standards and then convene representatives from each school, grade level, or content team to review and reach consensus. If teams utilize this process, there must be another feedback loop back to the teams before they determine final standards.

In some schools, teams do this work across grade levels and content areas. Individual teams of teachers can also determine essential standards. If individual teams determine essential standards, they must share and discuss their choices with the grade-level or course teams above and below theirs to ensure vertical alignment. Important questions to consider when discussing the essential standards include: If students come to you in the next course or year knowing and able to do *this*, how will this help or hinder you? How are you currently preparing students for the expectations in the list of priority standards?

Following is the five-step process for selecting essential standards. Begin with one section of the standards at a time. Times are approximate and for one section of the standards.

1. Individually decide (five to ten minutes). Each teacher decides the priorities utilizing the three criteria (endurance, leverage, and readiness).

2. Discuss where you agree or disagree (twenty to thirty minutes). Teams reach consensus by comparing their individual responses.

3. Review information from state or assessment consortium, such as blueprints, content frameworks, test specifications, and test content limits as well as any of your own pertinent data indicating your strengths and weakness (twenty to thirty minutes). Teams check to ensure the priorities align with the expectations of their state or national tests.

4. Chart initial priority standards (ten to fifteen minutes). Use chart paper, Google Docs, or a similar method.

5. Conduct vertical alignment and articulation (sixty to ninety minutes). This step involves examining the priority standards to determine gaps in learning, repetitions, omissions, and any overlaps by grade level or course. Are the standards more rigorous or complex as students matriculate up the grade levels and courses? Based on the state and national blueprints, is there an area that needs more or less emphasis?

Collaborative teams can use the chart in figure 3.2 (page 52) to record their selected standards. This helps teams gain greater clarity and plan for instruction and assessment.

Deconstruct Essential Standards to Identify Embedded Learning Targets

This process fosters deep understanding of the standards and agreement on proficiency. Teachers rarely teach an entire standard at one time or in one lesson. Instead, teams unwrap (or deconstruct) standards into smaller learning targets to determine the learning progression on the path to mastery of the essential standard. These smaller parts that underpin the priority standard become the basis for daily instruction, formative assessment, and interventions. Michelle Goodwin (2009) states, "A standard answers the question, where am I going in my learning? While learning targets show students the path to get there" (p. 90).

Learning targets are any achievement expectations for students on the path toward mastering a standard. They can be explicitly stated or implied. Teachers formally assess students on learning targets to monitor their progress and provide Tier 2 interventions along the way. The protocol for unwrapping the essential standards is a quick-and-easy three-step process, but just as is the case in determining which standards are essential, the collaborative dialogue the team engages in is the most important part of the process. It is during these discussions that a team builds shared knowledge and understanding of what each standard means and determines what each would look like when a student actually achieves it. Teachers become students of the standards they teach.

Teams complete the following three-step process to unwrap essential standards:

Take one standard.

↓

Unwrap or deconstruct it.

↓

Identify learning targets.

↓

Determine:
1. Formulative assessments—How many and when?
2. Flexible time to respond
3. Common assessments—What and when?

↓

Identify learning targets.

↓

Conduct formative assessments.

↓

Employ individual or team intervention.

↓

Conduct common summative assessment.

What Is It We Expect Students to Learn?

Grade: Subject: Semester: Team Members:

Description of Standard	Example of Rigor	Prerequisite Skills	When Taught	Common Summative Assessment	Extension Standards
What is the essential standard to be learned? Describe in student-friendly vocabulary.	What does proficient student work look like? Provide an example or description.	What prior knowledge, skills, or vocabulary are needed for a student to master this standard?	When will this standard be taught?	What assessments will be used to measure student mastery?	What will we do when students have already learned this standard?

Source: Adapted from Buffum et al., 2018, p. 88.

Figure 3.2: Essential standards chart.

Visit go.SolutionTree.com/RTIatWork for a free reproducible version of this figure.

1. Analyze and discuss the type of learning each essential standard requires of students.

2. Deconstruct each essential standard to identify the learning targets.

3. Convert learning targets into student-friendly language (Buffum et al., 2018, p. 90).

Analyze and Discuss the Type of Learning Each Essential Standard Requires of Students

Authors Jan Chappuis, Rick J. Stiggins, Steve Chappuis, and Judith Arter (2012) categorize standards and learning targets as knowledge, reasoning, performance skills, and product.

▽ **Knowledge:** Students know and understand concepts and facts. Students can find information they need. Key words that most often indicate knowledge standards include *explain, understand, describe, identify,* and *define.*

▽ **Reasoning:** Students use reasoning to solve a problem or make a decision. Key words that most often indicate reasoning standards include *compare, contrast, analyze, synthesize, classify, infer, deduce,* and *evaluate.*

▽ **Performance skills:** Students demonstrate that they can perform the process to complete a skill. Key words that most often indicate performance skill standards include *write, observe, listen, perform, do, use, question, conduct,* and *speak.*

▽ **Product:** Students use knowledge, reasoning, and performance skills to produce a quality product. Key words that most often indicate product standards include *design, produce, create, develop,* and *make.*

Teams should focus on the action or what the student is expected to do (the verb) to determine the type of standard.

Deconstruct Each Essential Standard to Identify the Learning Targets

Granular-sized learning targets are actually the focus of daily instruction and learning activities. For example, consider this English language arts–literacy ssential outcome: Students will "determine a theme or central idea of a text and how it is conveyed through particular details; provide a summary of the text distinct from personal opinions or judgments" (RL.6.2; NGA & CCSSO, 2010a, p. 36). Since students must provide a summary of the text, the overall standard is a product standard. In order to accomplish the standard, students must cover all four types of learning targets.

▽ **Knowledge:** Students will be able to define theme, central idea, details, summary, opinion, and judgement.

▽ **Reasoning:** Students will be able to determine a theme or central idea of a text. Students will be able to determine how the author conveys the theme or central idea through particular details.

▽ **Performance skills:** Students will be able to write a summary of the text.

▽ **Product:** Students will be able to produce a summary of the text distinct from personal opinion or judgments.

The purpose of deconstructing the standards is to clarify what the standards mean and build shared team understanding. Every teacher must be a master of the standards he or she teaches. This process ensures common learning expectations and that teachers are implementing a guaranteed and viable curriculum in every classroom regardless of who teaches the grade or course.

Convert Learning Targets Into Student-Friendly Language

The next critical step to engage students in owning their learning is to convert the learning targets into student-friendly language. Authors and consultants Sharon V. Kramer and Sarah Schuhl (2017) state:

> A teacher can tell a student what he or she has learned and not learned yet, as well as make a plan for continued learning, but the challenge is this: Can the student articulate what he or she has learned and not learned? If not, teachers may be working very hard to close a gap the student doesn't even know exists. Student learning targets bring students into the learning process. (p. 63).

Student-friendly learning targets are usually written in "I can" statements. Defining the critical terms in the process makes each target understandable but does not remove essential academic vocabulary. For example, in the previously deconstructed standard, the student-friendly learning targets would include the following.

▽ "I can define the terms *theme, central idea, details, summary, opinion,* and *judgement.*"

▽ "I can determine the theme or central idea of a text. I can determine how the author conveys the theme or central idea through details."

▽ "I can write a summary of the text."

▽ "I can produce a summary of the text without any personal opinions or judgements."

Students are often unintentionally left out of the learning process merely because they are not engaged from the very beginning. The only way students can partner with teachers in the learning process is to begin with clear learning targets. With clear targets, students can identify what they know and what they still need to learn. They can determine their next steps and self-assess or set goals likely to help them learn more. If students keep track of their learning targets throughout a unit of instruction, they will also know when they need additional time and support to learn. Tier 2 interventions are not a surprise or a punishment, but just the next step in the learning process. This is a growth mindset in action (Dweck, 2006)! A *growth mindset* fosters the belief that with effort and preparation, all students can learn.

Track Learning Progressions for Targeted Interventions

A *learning progression* consists of carefully sequenced steps involving the learning targets and prerequisite skills students must master to learn the standards. Learning progressions include learning targets or the bite-sized chunks of content that teachers teach on a daily basis and students must learn to master the essential standards.

Teachers must write this progression in student-friendly language and engage students in tracking their learning along the way. With learning progressions, teachers can determine exactly where students are in relation to mastering the targets or standards. This allows teachers to target the appropriate steps students need to accomplish for mastery. It is especially important as teachers and teams plan for targeted and specific interventions.

For example, a learning progression may contain these six steps for the sixth-grade standard RL.6.2 (NGA & CCSSO, 2010a, p. 36), as shown in figure 3.3.

Standard (learning progression ends with mastery of this standard): RL.6.2—Students will be able to determine a theme or central idea of a text and how it is conveyed through particular details; provide a summary of the text distinct from personal opinions or judgments.	
1	I can explain the meaning of *theme* and *central idea* and tell how the author lets the reader know.
2	I can determine a theme or central idea of a text.
3	I can explain the meaning of *conveyed* and *details*.
4	I can determine how the theme or central idea is conveyed through particular details. I can determine simple themes and details, working up to more complex in grade-level text.
5	I can describe the meaning of *summary*, *opinion*, and *judgment*.
6	I can write a summary of the text without personal opinions or judgments

Source for standard: NGA & CCSSO, 2010a, p. 36.

Figure 3.3: Learning progression for sixth-grade standard RL.6.2.

Teachers build learning progressions from the least complex or foundational concepts at step one and increase complexity as students complete steps two through six. This moves the learning from concrete to more abstract or least complex thinking to more complex thinking.

Teachers begin instruction at step 1 and proceed through the sequence of steps. Students track their progress, learning target by learning target, toward reaching the overall standard. As teachers monitor student progress, both teachers and students can easily determine each student's learning level to align targeted and specific interventions all along the way.

Without establishing the essential standards and deconstructing them collaboratively, what a student learns is left to each individual teacher's discretion. In addition, each teacher also determines the level of rigor or cognitive complexity. Making meaning of the standards and unwrapping (or deconstructing) them into teachable learning targets is the work of collaborative teams. Using this process, teachers build the concentrated instruction necessary to teach, assess, have data discussions, and provide Tier 2 interventions. It is the foundational process that ensures high levels of learning for all students.

Getting to targeted and specific Tier 2 interventions begins with unit planning. As teachers plan each unit in advance of actual instruction, they make meaning of the standards they expect students to learn, determine proficiency levels, deconstruct the standards into smaller learning targets, review the summative assessment to develop checkpoints, and analyze common formative assessment data to guide unit interventions and extensions. This preplanning process improves instruction because teachers understand the standards deeply and know the learning progression students must navigate to demonstrate proficiency and even higher levels of learning.

Teams work together to develop unit plans. Unit plans are not merely products teachers are expected to complete; instead, it is the process of creating unit plans that guides instruction, assessment, interventions, and learning extensions. The team discussion is more important than the actual document or protocol that guides the discussion.

Figure 3.4 is an example of an essential standards unit plan. Each team works through the protocol and uses a calendar to pace instruction, assessments, and interventions. This ensures timely assessment information and interventions at the point of need. In addition, for each unit plan the team decides SMART (strategic and specific, measurable, attainable, results oriented, and time bound; Conzemuis & O'Neill, 2014) goals. Based on data from previous years, teachers determine SMART goals that exceed previous results. For example, the end-of-unit assessment will conclude that 87 percent of grade 8 students are proficient on the unit three mathematics standards. The components of a unit plan allow teams to begin with the end in mind and get to targeted and specific interventions just in time.

Figure 3.5 (pages 57–58) contains a completed example of an English language arts essential standard unit plan for a ninth-grade standard. (The assessment component of this unit plan is the focus of the chapter 4, page 63.)

Complete the following plan.

Essential standard:			❑ Knowledge ❑ Reasoning	❑ Performance skills ❑ Product

End-of-unit assessment:			When taught: Instructional days needed:	

Knowledge Targets	Reasoning Targets	Performance Skills Targets	Product Targets	

Student-friendly learning targets:

Assessment (Which target or targets are being assessed? How will the assessment be used? Is it a common or individual assessment?)	Connection to Standard (How will this assessment set up students for successful mastery of the standard?)	Student Involvement (How will students engage in the assessment process?)	Time Line
1.			
2.			
3.			

Source: Buffum et al., 2018, pp. 94–95.

Figure 3.4: Essential standards unit plan.

*Visit **go.SolutionTree.com/RTIatWork** for a free reproducible version of this figure.*

Essential standard: W.9–10.1—Write arguments to support claims in an analysis of substantive topics or texts, using valid reasoning and relevant and sufficient evidence.	❑ Knowledge ❑ Reasoning	❑ Performance skills ☑ Product
End-of-unit assessment: Read an article on a contentious topic, and write a persuasive essay that includes an analysis of the topic. Then, take a stand and defend it with relevant and sufficient evidence. A choice of several articles will be provided.	When taught: November Instructional days needed: Nineteen	

Knowledge Targets	Reasoning Targets	Performance Skills Targets	Product Targets
• Organize essay and paragraph. • Demonstrate basic writing mechanics.	• Analyze text for key ideas. • Explain reasoning for stance taken. • Identify and include relevant and sufficient evidence. • Select and use persuasive language. • Sequence written text in a cohesive and organized manner.	• Demonstrate word processing skills. • Demonstrate understanding and use of all steps in the writing process.	• Write an effective introductory sentence. • Craft a cohesive, well-organized, and mechanically correct paragraph, text analysis, and support of a claim. • Draft multiple-paragraph essay.

Figure 3.5: Sample English language arts essential standards unit plan.

continued →

Student-friendly learning targets:
- I can analyze nonfiction text for key ideas.
- I can make a claim and use relevant and sufficient evidence to support it.
- I can organize and explain my ideas in writing.
- I can use correct spelling, punctuation, and grammar.
- I can explain my thinking and strategies.

Assessment (Which target or targets are being assessed? How will the assessment be used? Is it a common or individual assessment?)	Connection to Standard (How will this assessment set up students for successful mastery of the standard?)	Student Involvement (How will students engage in the assessment process?)	Time Line
1. Mascot persuasive paragraph (common formative, individual)	Students demonstrate baseline persuasive writing skills.	Students self-assess and set goals for improving persuasive writing skills.	Day three
2. Text analysis paragraph (formative and summative, individual)	Students practice comprehension and analysis of text, as well as paragraph organization.	Students self-assess and peer-assess the pretest and revise.	Day six: Rough draft Day eight: Final draft
3. Mechanics quiz and paragraph editing (summative, individual)	Students develop accurate use of mechanics and ability to self-edit.	Students analyze quiz results to identify growth targets.	Day ten
4. Practice essay (formative, individual and partner classes)	Students combine all skills in a finished product.	Students peer-assess and collaboratively score sample papers.	Days eleven through fifteen

Source: Buffum et al., 2018, pp. 98–99.
Source for standard: NGA & CCSSO, 2010a, p. 45.

Conclusion

The information in this chapter set the foundation for getting to targeted and specific interventions. Tier 2 interventions are based on the essential standards that students are expected to know and be able to do. Without a clear pathway to this learning, it would be difficult and even impossible to understand the misconceptions that get in the way of student learning. Tier 2 interventions begin here.

The "Chapter 3: Key Considerations Rubric" reproducibles on pages 60–61 serve as a touchstone for schools and teams to evaluate their current reality and inspire conversations regarding areas of strength for the team or school, areas to focus on, and next steps. Teams can use this simple rubric during team meetings or with the whole faculty as a way to foster discussions about implementing effective RTI in their school.

Big Ideas for Chapter 3

The following six big ideas provide an overview of the most important concepts from this chapter.

1. The prerequisite to targeted and specific Tier 2 interventions is for collaborative teacher teams to be in absolute agreement on what students should know and be able to do.

2. It is impossible to teach all the state or district standards for each grade level or course. Teacher teams must determine which of the standards are most essential for students to know deeply.

3. The essential standards for each grade level or course are the critical learning expectations teachers teach students to mastery, assess to ensure students have learned, have data conversations about, and provide Tier 2 interventions for those students needing additional time and support to learn.

4. Teacher teams must deconstruct essential standards into smaller student learning targets on the pathway to understanding an entire standard. Teachers must also share these learning targets with students in student-friendly language to engage *them* during the entire process.

5. Determining the learning progression of each standard provides a road map for learning that clearly identifies where students may need more help and support.

6. Teacher teams should use an essential standards unit plan to assist members as they discuss instructional strategies and schedule assessments along the way.

Chapter 3: Key Considerations Rubric

Directions: With your school or team, read the key considerations listed in the far-left column of the rubric. Evaluate where your team or school currently is and what steps you need to establish in your daily practice to achieve these goals. Once completed, with your team discuss your areas of strength, areas of challenge, and next steps for your school or team.

Embedded

This is how we do business. We do this without thinking about it; it's just part of our school or team culture.

Developing

We get it and do fairly well in implementing this into our daily work.

Limited

We have some individuals in our school or team who understand and implement this, but it's sporadic at best.

No Evidence

There is little to no evidence of this; we have work to do!

Key Considerations	Embedded	Developing	Limited	No Evidence
We have mapped common expectations (essential standards) for the curriculum for the entire school year.				
Teachers at the same grade level and in the same content area teach the same units at the same time using a common pacing guide.				
Teams have a shared understanding of what each essential standard means and what it looks like when a student demonstrates it at the proficient level or higher.				

page 1 of 2

Key Considerations	Embedded	Developing	Limited	No Evidence
Instruction aligns with the level of rigor each essential standard and learning target requires.				
What students must learn and be able to do is clearly articulated and guaranteed for every level of every course.				

An area of **strength** for us:

An area of **challenge** for us:

Our **next steps**:

page 2 of 2

Using Data to Target Tier 2 Interventions

It is assessment which helps us distinguish between teaching and learning.

—Douglas Fisher and Nancy Frey

A Story From Washington High School

The administration at Washington High School was very excited to begin its intervention period. Administrators had successfully created a schedule that included time for interventions during the regular school day twice per week. The administration involved the entire staff in carving out the time. They built shared understanding regarding the rationale and clearly articulated the need for interventions. Finally, teachers had the time to support and help the struggling students keep up with the curriculum. Teachers decided to provide interventions by sharing the students who needed help with the same content. After the first month of implementation, it was clear that there was confusion and challenges they had not anticipated. The principal asked the leadership team to bring the concerns to a meeting for the purpose of discussing possible solutions.

As the meeting began, one of the teachers immediately said, "This is a mess, and it will never work!"

Another teacher said she was overwhelmed with the number of students she was supposed to be helping. Others chimed in with several other issues. The principal asked each teacher to describe his or her experience with the intervention time thus far.

As everyone listened, it became clear that a critical step in the process was missing. Student identification for interventions was inconsistent and worse—not tied to assessment data. One teacher assigned a student to interventions because he did not complete his homework assignment. Another teacher assigned a student to interventions because her mom called and wanted her to raise her grade from a B+ to an A. Yet another teacher assigned a student to interventions because he failed the last test.

The teachers who had agreed to do the interventions were at a loss on how to help all these students with differing needs. It was obvious these teachers needed more detailed and specific information on each student and there was not an established, consistent method for assigning students to interventions.

Teachers should determine Tier 2 interventions by analyzing data from the end-of-unit assessment as well as the team-developed common formative assessments and teacher checks for understanding that lead up to the unit test. Teams then converge the information from these assessments to determine the specific cause of the learning problem in order to deliver a targeted response. As these data discussions occur, teams also dig deep to determine which strategy was more effective in ensuring students learned. It may be that one teacher's results are better than other team members' results. Therefore, teachers should use the strategy that garnered the best results for instruction during interventions. Often, the teacher with the best results is also the best person to deliver the intervention in that specific area.

Washington High School left out a critical step in the process of delivering targeted and specific Tier 2 interventions. As we establish in chapter 3 (page 43), it is fundamental to be clear on the essential standards and learning targets that students need to know and be able to do on a unit-by-unit basis. Without collaboratively organizing and analyzing assessment data, the interventions will be random and the learning expectations unclear.

This chapter will explain *why* we need to do things differently when using data to target Tier 2 interventions and offer specific strategies and tools for *how* to get there.

Why We Need to Do Things Differently

This scenario plays out all too often in schools. Teams must base interventions on data—and not just any data, but targeted data that reveals the misconceptions students need clarified. This requires teams develop a common end-of-unit assessment that gives them the information to diagnose specific student needs. The purpose of assessment is not merely to measure learning but also to determine how to help students learn more. This is especially true for Tier 2 interventions since the intent is to ensure students are proficient in the grade level or course-specific essential standards. The more specific the information teachers can glean from the data, the more targeted the interventions can become, which leads to more learning in the least amount of time. The purpose of assessment for Tier 2 interventions is to know what to do next to ensure all students learn at high levels.

End-of-unit assessments are part of an assessment system that supports learning. In the traditional instruction-assessment cycle, teachers begin a unit of instruction and teach, teach, teach, assess, and assign a grade. In most situations, this approach leads to results that indicate some students have not learned enough to be successful. In addition, most teachers feel a compelling need to move on in the curriculum to adhere to a pacing guide or just because there is so much to teach. When asked, teachers say their intent is to reteach the content students did not learn, but they still need to move on.

Let's consider this approach from a students' standpoint. What is the likelihood that the student who struggled to learn unit one will be able to relearn that unit's concepts while simultaneously keeping up with the class as they work through unit two? We all know the answer to that question. It is impossible for most students, especially those who struggle, to learn the content the first time. When we approach assessment and interventions in this manner on a regular basis, we create remediation because it becomes impossible for students to keep up. In fact, most fall farther and farther behind. Once students get into a remediation cycle, it is almost impossible for them to break out. Schools still utilize this approach, but it actually creates the need for remediation. So is there a more effective way to ensure learning for all? What instruction-assessment cycle promotes learning? How can we catch students before they need remediation?

Here's How

Getting to targeted and specific interventions begins with creating a system that supports learning. The process starts with state standards not because we necessarily agree with them or believe they are written well or clearly, but because they are the road map to the state assessments. Teachers would never give an assessment if they did not teach the concepts and skills prior. It would be unfair to test students on the state assessments without teaching the required standards. The standards are the only pathway to the test. We have determined the essential standards, now what? Following are the next steps to ensure targeted and specific Tier 2 interventions.

▽ Deconstruct state standards into specific learning targets.

▽ Determine the appropriate assessments.

▽ Establish how to use and analyze data.

Deconstruct State Standards Into Specific Learning Targets

Teams determine the most essential standards from the state documents and deconstruct them into specific learning targets. They must determine the level of rigor, or depth of knowledge (DOK), for each learning target to be sure students will be able to interact with the content at the level of complexity the standard requires. DOK is a scale from one to four that provides the highest level of thinking for each standard and accompanying test item (Francis, 2016).

After determining the most essential standards and DOK of the learning targets, teams develop the end-of-unit assessment, along with the common formative assessments and checks for understanding to use along the path to learning the essential standards. After each type of assessment or check-in, there is an opportunity for re-engaging their thinking or reteaching before students get too far behind.

The assessment intervention system in figure 4.1 describes the steps necessary to ensure all students are successful on the assessments, in the next grade or course, and life beyond school. At each step there is an opportunity to provide more time and support for student learning. This assessment and intervention system supports student learning.

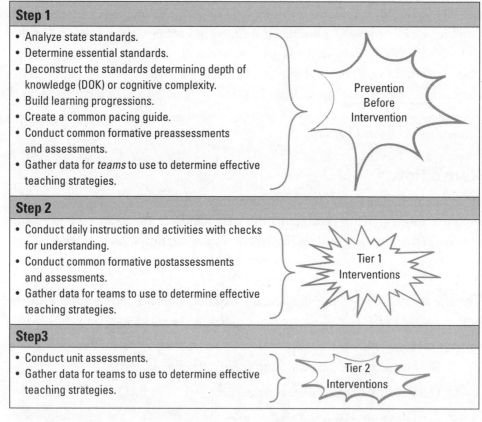

Step 1
- Analyze state standards.
- Determine essential standards.
- Deconstruct the standards determining depth of knowledge (DOK) or cognitive complexity.
- Build learning progressions.
- Create a common pacing guide.
- Conduct common formative preassessments and assessments.
- Gather data for *teams* to use to determine effective teaching strategies.

Prevention Before Intervention

Step 2
- Conduct daily instruction and activities with checks for understanding.
- Conduct common formative postassessments and assessments.
- Gather data for teams to use to determine effective teaching strategies.

Tier 1 Interventions

Step3
- Conduct unit assessments.
- Gather data for teams to use to determine effective teaching strategies.

Tier 2 Interventions

Source: Kramer, 2014.

Figure 4.1: Assessment intervention system.

As teachers work through this instruction-assessment-intervention cycle, students get help *before* they get too far behind. For example, the plan is to re-engage student thinking on fractions during the fractions unit, not when the entire class has moved on to geometry. This creates a safety net for students and fills gaps before remediation takes hold.

Collaborative teams design Tier 2 interventions at the learning target level, not for the entire standard. Team members should ask, "Which parts of the standard are causing students to struggle?" This ensures that intervention activities aim at the specific misconceptions getting in the way of students learning the standards.

Along the way, it is important to create assessments that will yield *instructionally actionable data*. This means creating or selecting test items that match the targets and standards in content and rigor and mirror the requirements of the types of tests students will take at the district and state levels. In addition, the test questions and possible distractors should contain common misconceptions so teams can discern exactly what each student needs to move his or her learning forward. For example, a mathematics problem that asks students to find the mode of a given set of numbers should also include the mean and median as two of the distractors. This helps teachers identify students who are not clear on the difference among *mean*, *mode*, and *median*. Test developers use distractors that contain common errors to raise the rigor level of the actual test item.

Once a collaborative team determines the learning targets and standards to include in the common formative and end-of-unit assessments, it must determine the appropriate assessments.

Determine the Appropriate Assessments

It's important for teams to decide which types of assessments are best for evaluating what students know and where they are in their learning progression. Assessments fall into the categories of selected response, constructed response, performance, or personal communication (Stiggins et al., 2006; Vagle, 2015).

Selected Response

Selected-response assessments usually take the form of multiple choice, fill in the blank, matching, true-false, or answers containing a few words. These types of questions elicit right or wrong answers, which makes grading easier but less open to analyzing errors. In fact, it is sometimes difficult to determine whether the student guessed and was just lucky that day. It is also difficult to assess strategic thinking and reasoning utilizing these types of items. If written at higher levels of rigor, multiple-choice questions can be some of the most difficult to construct. Ideally, each distractor or incorrect answer gives a teacher as much information as the correct answer because each distractor represents a common misconception. This allows teachers to re-engage student thinking at the point of specific need.

Constructed Response

Constructed-response assessments are typically short answers or essays using sentences, completing a graphic organizer, showing work in mathematics problems, or explaining and justifying a response. These assessments tend to be easier to write but more time consuming to score. There is a need to ensure scoring is consistent from teacher to teacher as well. Teachers use constructed-response items to assess reasoning and thinking.

Performance

Performance assessments refer to demonstrations or actual performances students give or products students create, such as giving speeches, playing musical instruments, or writing essays. These types of assessments require a clear, consistent rubric that actually measures proficiency on multiple criteria. In addition, each teacher must apply the rubric in exactly the same manner to garner reliable, actionable data.

Personal Communication

Personal-communication assessments are one-to-one opportunities to determine student proficiency on specific targets or standards. This type of assessment occurs as teachers meet with students in interviews or to conduct writing conferences. Personal-communication assessments are underutilized mainly because it is difficult to determine proficiency since teachers prompt discussions and conversations in different ways and the discussions can meander. They can also be subjective if the teachers do not agree on the criteria they will accept and the exact manner to administer the assessments. This type of assessment should include detailed directions and scripted prompts that the entire team adheres to.

There is value in developing assessments that contain items in a couple of categories. Teams need to let the learning target or standard determine the type of test item that will accurately measure a student's proficiency. The test items can come from any source available to teachers, such as textbooks, item banks, released items from state and national assessments, and teacher-written test questions. Teams must carefully select or write items that match the target and standard at the required rigor level and will yield instructionally actionable data. Table 4.1 outlines which methods work best to assess the different types of learning targets.

As teams design their common formative and end-of-unit assessments, they should consider each of the following questions.

- ▸ How well do the items on the assessment match the standard's intended rigor?
- ▸ How well does the assessment method match the assessed standard?
- ▸ How well has the team represented each essential learning target on the assessment?
- ▸ How clear are the directions?
- ▸ How will the team commonly score the assessment? (Kramer & Schuhl, 2017, p. 88)

Table 4.1: Methods for Assessing Learning Targets

Target to Assess	Assessment Method			
	Selected Response	Constructed Response	Performance	Personal Communication
Knowledge	Multiple choice, true-false, matching, and fill in the blank can determine mastery of elements of knowledge	Essay exercises can tap understanding of relationships among elements of knowledge	Not a good choice for this target	Can ask student questions, evaluate answers, and infer mastery—but a time-consuming option
Reasoning Proficiency	Can assess understanding of basic patterns of reasoning	Written descriptions of complex-problem solutions can provide a window into reasoning proficiency	Can watch students solve problems and infer about reasoning proficiency	Can ask student to think aloud or ask follow-up questions to probe reasoning proficiency
Performance Skills	Can assess mastery of the prerequisites of skillful performance but cannot tap the skill itself—not a good choice for this target	Can assess mastery of the prerequisites of skillful performance but cannot tap the skill itself—not a good choice for this target	Can observe and evaluate skills as they are performed	Strong match when skill is oral communication proficiency; also can assess mastery of knowledge prerequisite to skillful performance
Ability to Create Products	Can assess mastery of knowledge prerequisite to the ability to create quality products but cannot assess the quality of products themselves—not a good choice for this target	Can assess mastery of knowledge prerequisite to the ability to create quality products, but cannot assess the quality of products themselves—not a good choice for this target	A strong match; can assess: 1. Proficiency in carrying out steps in product development 2. Attributes of the product itself	Can probe procedural knowledge and knowledge of attributes of quality products but cannot assess product quality

Source: Adapted from Stiggens et al., 2006, p. 100.

Teams must also consider how students and teachers will respond to the assessment results by asking, "Will these items give us enough specific information to know how to respond in the most effective and efficient manner so that all students will learn?" (Kramer & Schuhl, 2017).

Establish How to Use and Analyze Data

Terry Wilhelm (2011, as cited in Mense & Crain-Dorough, 2017) states, "Many schools are the victims of being data rich and information poor (DRIP)" (p. 30). We agree. It is not about collecting data; it is about turning data into usable information that leads to instructional actions. As we work with teams across North America, it is obvious teachers are inundated with state assessment data, district assessment data, schoolwide measures, and summative and common formative assessment data points. So, now what? What do we do with these data?

Since the purpose for each assessment is different, it is necessary to create a balanced system of assessments that includes both summative and formative measures. To describe the difference between these two types of assessments, consider this analogy. Imagine that *formative assessment* is an ongoing video of the learning process. As teachers and students engage in the learning process, they are gathering information along the way to ensure that learning is taking place. A *summative assessment*, on the other hand, is a snapshot or still photograph of learning at a particular point in time, usually a culmination of a specific course of study like a semester or final exam or the state assessment. While teachers use summative assessments to measure learning, they use formative assessments to diagnose learning in order to ensure *all* students learn.

A balanced assessment system provides multiple opportunities to inform learning through the formative process (ongoing video) marked with a periodic summative assessment (photograph). Each of these types of assessment serves a different purpose and are important to obtain a complete picture of student learning. Even the most summative assessments (such as ACT, SAT, PISA, or state-administered standardized assessments) have a place in a balanced system. Summative assessments assist schools, districts, and states to calibrate the curriculum and instruction to ensure all students are prepared to compete in the future. These assessments offer a point of comparison that would be difficult to determine without the results of a broad-based assessment.

Figure 4.2 shows a balanced assessment system. The most summative types of tests are standardized and usually external. Standardized tests give information teachers use to determine whether curriculum, assessment, instructional strategies, and pacing are appropriate. End-of-course assessments take the form of final exams or projects and are more summative since teachers administer them at the end of the course.

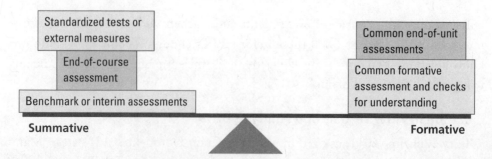

Figure 4.2: Balanced assessment system.

The purpose of summative assessments is to issue a grade; they will also indicate a need for further remediation or course recovery. Benchmark or district assessments are also more summative, and teachers typically administer them quarterly, at the end of a trimester, or every six weeks. Teachers use these assessments at each school site or throughout the district to analyze curriculum alignment, instructional impact, and pacing. Benchmark assessments also allow teams to provide Tier 2 interventions for students still experiencing difficulty. Teams create common summative assessments to determine a grade or "snapshot of learning" at a particular point in time. Teachers should administer these assessments when they are sure most students have learned the essential standards.

In contrast, teachers can create common formative assessments containing mini-tasks they assess with rubrics, short quizzes, and common writing prompts during a unit of instruction. These also include team-developed end-of-unit assessments teachers score to determine who needs Tier 2 interventions and on which specific essential standard or learning target. This is an opportunity for teams to develop interventions by essential standard, learning target, student, and need.

Finally, the most formative assessments are those teachers do daily as they check for understanding in each lesson. These can take the form of questioning, quick written responses, clickers, whiteboard activities, exit tickets, and student conferences. Checking for understanding during the instructional process gives students immediate feedback on learning and teachers data for adjusting instruction and learning strategies. It is just-in-time teaching and learning.

Whatever the form of evidence, it is the action both teachers and students take that makes assessment formative and powerful. The greatest impact of formative assessment on teachers is the diagnostic information they garner to use to modify instruction (Popham, 2011). In addition, these assessments are typically unobtrusive, which means they do not interrupt the learning process (Marzano, 2010). In fact, they are an integral component of learning. The impact for students is the ability to clearly understand their mistakes so they can re-examine their thinking at the point of need or just in time (before they get too far behind). According to assessment consultant and author Dylan Wiliam (2011, 2018), formative assessment practices double the speed of student learning.

Formative assessment processes require two additional components. An assessment is not formative unless students are involved from the beginning of the instructional process and receive meaningful feedback (Moss & Brookhart, 2009). According to Reeves (2016) in *FAST Grading: A Guide to Implementing Best Practices*, feedback must be fair, accurate, specific, and timely (FAST). Feedback must cause thinking (Wiliam, 2011), and the most critical feedback is from students to teachers, not teachers to students (Marzano, 2007, 2017). This critical feedback is an opportunity for students to describe their thinking and for teachers to respond in a way that moves the learning forward. However, when teachers deliver feedback, the most important aspect is for students to take action.

This requires students be involved in their own learning from the beginning of a unit of instruction. The shift is from *teacher-directed* to *student-directed* learning. The intent is not just student engagement but student *ownership* of their learning. The only way we can expect students to own their learning is to include them from the beginning.

Kramer and Schuhl (2017) offer some strategies to engage students in learning from the beginning of the unit, not just when it's time to take the end-of-unit assessment. Utilizing these strategies, teachers and students become partners in learning:

- Students name their learning targets.
- Students manage their materials and data and track their progress.
- Students set goals and learning plans or activities for themselves.
- Students self-assess their work.
- Students reflect on what they have learned and make connections to new learning.
- Students generate possible test items at appropriate rigor levels.
- Students participate in rubric development.
- Students engage in meaningful dialogue about their learning.
- Students support each other in addressing learning gaps. (p. 52)

As teams plan each unit of instruction, the process must include expectations for student involvement. Teams should consider the following questions during the planning process.

▽ What are the student learning targets for this unit? (Write them using "I can" statements.)

▽ How will students know the learning target for each lesson?

▽ Where and how will students record their reflections during the learning process (for example, use a tracker sheet, quantify the path to learning the target, or writing goals along the way)?

▽ What will students use as evidence of learning (for example, exit tickets, quizzes, homework, classwork, online resources)?

▽ How will the team teach students how to reflect and monitor their learning during the unit?

Teachers use formative data to analyze learning and plan interventions. Timing is everything. Tier 2 interventions should occur as close to first best instruction as possible. This means analyzing learning information and data must be fast, nimble, and follow a specific process or protocol. Using a protocol creates a safe environment to discuss the data and ensures the timeliness of the intervention.

It is important for teams to organize data in a way that allows for purposeful discussion. The data protocol in figure 4.3 can help guide a team's purposeful discussions.

1. Determine the percentage of students proficient on the assessment for each standard or target by teacher and then for all students within the team. Write the information in the following chart.				
	Target 1	**Target 2**	**Target 3**	**Target 4**
Teacher A				
Teacher B				
Teacher C				
Teacher D				
Total Team				

2. For each standard or target, determine the number of students who are proficient, close to proficient, and far from proficient by teacher and as a team (write the number or the names of the students).				
Target 1				
	Proficient	**Close to Proficient**	**Far From Proficient**	**Total**
Teacher A				
Teacher B				
Teacher C				
Teacher D				
Total Team				
Target 2				
	Proficient	**Close to Proficient**	**Far From Proficient**	**Total**
Teacher A				
Teacher B				
Teacher C				
Teacher D				
Total Team				

Figure 4.3: Data-analysis protocol.

continued →

Target 3				
	Proficient	**Close to Proficient**	**Far From Proficient**	**Total**
Teacher A				
Teacher B				
Teacher C				
Teacher D				
Total Team				

Target 4				
	Proficient	**Close to Proficient**	**Far From Proficient**	**Total**
Teacher A				
Teacher B				
Teacher C				
Teacher D				
Total Team				

1. What skills did the proficient students demonstrate in their work that set their work apart? Which instructional strategies did teachers use that effectively produced those results?

2. In which area or areas did my students struggle? In which areas did our team's students struggle? What is the cause? How will we respond? Which strategies will we try next?

3. Which students need additional time and support to learn the standards or targets? What is our plan?

4. Which students need extension and enrichment? What is our plan?

5. Do these data show we are on track to meet our SMART goal? Why or why not?

Source: Kramer & Schuhl, 2017, pp. 103–104.

Each teacher enters his or her own data, typically using the team's shared Google doc. At the team meeting, members then analyze the information. In step 1 of the protocol, teachers capture students' overall proficiency levels and specific targets. These are the overall results for each class and the team. In step 2, teachers determine the number (and names) of students in each class who were far from proficient, close to proficient, or proficient on each learning target. This growth measure can assist students and teachers in moving students from one level to the next. It is also a way to help students foster a growth mindset (Dweck, 2006). As students grow, proficiency levels increase.

The guiding questions in figure 4.3 (pages 73–74) examine student strengths and areas of need on a deeper level than right or wrong. As teams discuss questions three through seven, members begin to determine the types of errors students are making to fully understand the misconceptions students must clarify as they reach mastery of the targets. In addition, teams investigate the most effective strategies and approaches to teaching. This is *not* to see who the best teacher is but instead a data-mining opportunity to determine the best strategy to ensure more students initially learn at high levels. If interventions are specific and robust, teams need to clearly understand exactly what misconceptions are getting in the way of student learning. This can only be ascertained as teams conduct an error analysis and discuss the types of errors students are making and why. Error analysis ensures teams get to the root cause of the problem.

To illustrate this team process, figure 4.4 shows an example of a mathematics standard and the accompanying assessment items. Although this is a simple example, the analysis process works at all grade levels and in every content area.

Mathematics standard: Use place value understanding to round multidigit whole numbers to any place limited to whole numbers less than or equal to 1,000,000.

Sample assessment items:

1. Round 23,456 to the nearest hundred.

2. Carla rounded the number of students in her school to the nearest hundred. She said there were about 500 students in her school. What is the largest number of students that could be in her school? Use pictures, numbers, words, or all three to explain how you know your answer is correct.

3. Cameron has 4,561 baseball cards, and Jesse has 4,612 baseball cards. Cameron said he can round their number of baseball cards to the same value. Is Cameron correct? Explain how you know.

Source: Adapted from Schuhl, 2017.
Source for standard: NGA & CCSSO, 2010b.

Figure 4.4: Assessment items for mathematics standard.

After team members create assessment items, they need to decide the necessary steps to deliver a collective response. To do this, they must agree on how they will score and administer the assessment and decide how to analyze the data to determine trends in student work and what the team will do next to re-engage all learners.

Author and consultant Sarah Schuhl (2017) offers the following four-step plan for responding to assessment results.

1. The team decides on the scoring agreements by determining the criteria or expectation for each category in the data-analysis protocol.

2. Each teacher sorts student work into the categories *far from proficient* to *proficient* and include a category for students who demonstrate advanced knowledge or thinking. Individual teachers should come to the team meeting prepared to discuss results with the entire team.

3. For each category, the team identifies common understandings, common errors, misunderstandings, and misconceptions. As the team examines the trends and types of errors in student work, they note them by category—far from proficient, close to proficient, proficient, and advanced—and the discussion leads to a deeper understanding of students' errors and misconceptions. Figure 4.5 is an example of the possible trends in student work aligned to the mathematics standard and the assessment items.

Far From Proficient	Close to Proficient	Proficient	Advanced
• Rounds to the incorrect place value • Unable to explain answers • For item 2, writes several large numbers as the answer • For item 3, chooses the largest number of cards; some explain why 4,512 > 4,561	• Rounds the values correctly • Unable to explain answers using a picture or words; simply restates the numbers • Unable to use names of place value when explaining rounding in item 3	• Able to round correctly • Rounding explanations only include a rule for rounding up or down (for example, it is a 6, so round up)	• Able to round correctly • Rounding explanations include place value language and number lines

Source: Adapted from Schuhl, 2017.

Figure 4.5: Trends in student work.

4. The team considers the strengths and weaknesses evident in student work to determine the implications for future instruction as well as the specific instruction or experiences it will design for students. The team determines the specific intervention or extension of learning for each group. It then decides on a collective response to move the *far from proficenct* and *close to proficient* groups to *proficient*, and provides learning extentions for the *proficient* and *advanced* groups.

Now teams can group students by common errors and the causes of those misconceptions, not just by levels or right and wrong answers. This process not only saves time during interventions but also fosters a growth mindset in students (Dweck, 2006). Students might respond to wrong answers like, "I can't do this" or worse, "I'm just dumb."

Teachers and students can turn around negative comments, feelings, and emotions when they look deeply at the work and begin to re-engage their thinking. Teachers might say, "It looks like you know how to round numbers correctly, but you may have been confused about place value. Tell me how you solved this problem." This approach communicates a message of positive movement toward mastery. It honors student learning, even if students are not quite to mastery *yet*. It is the way to build confidence and self-efficacy in students and at the same time, makes them aware of their thinking at the conceptual level. This positive message is possible when teams have carefully analyzed the data to determine the most efficient and effective way to deliver Tier 2 interventions while partnering with students.

Conclusion

As we think back to the Washington High School scenario at the beginning of this chapter, it is now easy to see what steps we can take to ensure time spent on Tier 2 interventions is as productive and powerful as it should be. If the goal is truly *learning for all*, then the most targeted and specific Tier 2 interventions are at the core of the work. In the end, it is not about putting a grade in the gradebook, it is about *learning*. Most schools have a culture of grading, not a culture of learning. The strategies in this chapter offer a shift in thinking to a true culture of learning.

The "Chapter 4: Key Considerations Rubric" reproducibles on pages 79–80 serve as a touchstone for schools and teams to evaluate their current reality and inspire conversations regarding areas of strength for the team or school, areas to focus on, and next steps. Teams can use this simple rubric during team meetings or with the whole faculty as a way to foster discussions about implementing effective RTI in their school.

Big Ideas for Chapter 4

The following seven big ideas provide an overview of the most important concepts from this chapter.

1. The essential purpose of assessment is not to merely measure learning but to determine how to help students learn more.

2. A balanced assessment system with both summative and formative measures provides a comprehensive account of the learning process.

3. Teachers can use formative assessment measures to deliver Tier 1 and 2 interventions in an RTI system of supports.

4. Schools are inundated with data but unless teachers turn data into information that leads to instructional actions, it is meaningless.

5. Teachers begin by designing assessments that provide instructionally actionable data. They select and write items to include the required rigor of the essential standards and provide insight into the conceptual understanding of each student.

6. Data-analysis protocols are an efficient and effective way for teams to discuss data and determine the specific needs of each student. Data analysis must include an error-analysis component to deeply understand the root cause of misconceptions.

7. An assessment is not formative unless students are engaged in the process from the beginning. In this process, the goal is for students to own their learning in partnership with their teachers.

Chapter 4: Key Considerations Rubric

Directions: With your school or team, read the key considerations listed in the far-left column of the rubric. Evaluate where your team or school currently is and what steps you need to establish in your daily practice to achieve these goals. Once completed, with your team discuss your areas of strength, areas of challenge, and next steps for your school or team.

Embedded

This is how we do business. We do this without thinking about it; it's just part of our school or team culture.

Developing

We get it and do fairly well in implementing this into our daily work.

Limited

We have some individuals in our school or team who understand and implement this, but it's sporadic at best.

No Evidence

There is little to no evidence of this; we have work to do!

Key Considerations	Embedded	Developing	Limited	No Evidence
Our school or district has created common formative and summative assessments in a balanced system.				
Teams create common end-of-unit assessments and formative measures before beginning a unit of instruction.				
Teams create assessments that align with the rigor of the essential standards and use the most appropriate method to assess.				

page 1 of 2

Key Considerations	Embedded	Developing	Limited	No Evidence
Teams obtain data in a format they can analyze in a timely manner to target Tier 2 interventions.				
Teams use a data protocol to guide the data discussion, including a specific method for analyzing common errors and misconceptions that lead to actions.				
Teams group students for Tier 2 interventions by common misconceptions and errors at the conceptual level of understanding.				

An area of **strength** for us:

An area of **challenge** for us:

Our **next steps**:

page 2 of 2

Implementing Powerful Instructional Supports

The greatest impact on learning is the daily lived experiences of students in classrooms, and that is determined much more by how teachers teach than by what they teach.

—Dylan Wiliam

A Story From Jefferson Middle School

The eighth-grade team at Jefferson Middle School analyzed data from a unit common assessment to determine which students needed more time and support to learn the essential standards. During the discussion, it became evident that some students' errors were a result of misconceptions that team members needed to address.

As the team leader, Mr. Jameson, interacted with the team, one of the teachers declared, "OK, so you said that a Tier 2 intervention is not more of the same, and we should use a different strategy to reteach. I understand that if the first way we introduced and taught a concept did not work, it probably won't work to do it the same way again, even if we do it louder and slower. But honestly, I used my best strategy the first time. It's not like I saved it for reteaching. How do I now re-engage student thinking in a whole new way?"

One of the greatest challenges teams face is responding to the academic diversity in classrooms. The question teacher teams most frequently ask is, "How do we support the needs of all learners?" This question is usually followed by: "What new and comprehensive strategies can we use to re-engage students and extend learning since we used the best strategy the first time we taught this?" "How do we find the time to do interventions and also keep up with the pacing of the curriculum?" and "How will we extend learning for some students while we respectfully re-engage others?" These are practicalities teams deal with on a regular basis as they plan to respond to student learning with Tier 2 interventions.

It is evident from this scenario that teachers often revert to just going over the test and calling that an intervention. This practice is especially counterproductive when teachers do it with the entire class, even with those students who learned it the first time. It is also generally not helpful to students who do not understand the concept because this practice does not re-engage their thinking at the conceptual level. This practice merely tells students which answers are right and which are wrong. It is not an intervention practice that ensures learning or transfer to more complex thinking.

Clearly, the team at Jefferson did not have a plan for interventions or extensions. Teams need to be intentional about answering all four PLC critical questions during the unit-planning process prior to teaching the unit. This includes identifying additional ways to teach specific learning targets. When teams have these discussions prior to beginning a unit, they are taking a proactive (rather than reactive) approach to student learning. As teams review data during the unit, members discuss their original plan for interventions and determine the best way to teach so students will learn at a deep conceptual level.

This chapter will explain *why* we need to do things differently when implementing powerful instructional supports and offers specific strategies and tools for *how* to make it happen.

Why We Need to Do Things Differently

Even with the best lesson designs that include classroom engagement and differentiation, some teachers will still have students who need additional time and support to learn at high levels. Teams should schedule this additional support systematically during the school day. Chapter 6 (page 95) includes sample schedules that demonstrate how schools have arranged time for Tier 2 interventions.

It turns out that interventions and learning extensions go hand in hand. The manner in which teachers plan interventions and extensions must honor the learning that has occurred with respectful tasks. By *respectful*, we mean tasks that honor student learning. We do not honor their learning when we give students who demonstrate proficiency more of the same work. These students need work that is an extension of what they have already learned. In the same way, when teachers approach reteaching as a do-over for students (instead of addressing specific misconceptions), they are not honoring students' learning.

The goal is to plan respectful tasks with high expectations for all students and activities that equally engage each learner. Respectful tasks honor student learning and build on what students know at all levels. While reteaching involves teaching the lesson again, re-engaging analyzes student errors and missteps and asks students to revisit their thinking. In a similar manner, a learning extension applies the core learning and asks students to demonstrate learning the teacher has not directly taught.

As discussed in chapter 4 (page 63), it is important to identify trends in student work to strategically target a skill or concept to grow student learning. In *Simplifying Response to Intervention*, Buffum et al. (2012) state, "The more targeted the intervention, the more likely it will work. Most schools' interventions are ineffective because they are too broad in focus and rarely address a child's individual learning needs" (p. 136).

Here's How

So the more teams know about the types of errors and the thinking behind those errors, the quicker and easier interventions become. After giving a common formative or summative assessment, identify those students by target (far from proficient, close to proficient, proficient, or advanced). Bring samples of student work to the collaborative team meeting to share with other members the work of students who have demonstrated in each category. This will help teams determine the needs of each student for structural re-engagement. It also allows for grouping students with like or similar needs for interventions. This is the most effective and efficient manner to deliver Tier 2 interventions that ensure high levels of learning for all students.

To ensure that teams can effectively implement powerful instruction supports for *all* students:

▽ Implement re-engagement strategies

▽ Extend students who are already proficient

Implement Re-Engagement Strategies

What new and comprehensive strategies can we use to re-engage students and extend learning, since we use the best strategy the first time we teach a concept? There are many effective instructional practices to use at various grade levels and within different subject areas. Robert J. Marzano, Debra J. Pickering, and Jane E. Pollock (2001) identify nine categories of instructional strategies that affect student achievement. Through their research utilizing meta-analysis that combines the results of many studies, they were able to determine nine strategies that had the greatest average effect on student achievement.

1. Identify similarities and differences

2. Summarize and take notes

3. Reinforce effort and provide recognition

4. Provide homework and practice

5. Encourage nonlinguistic representations

6. Include cooperative learning

7. Set objectives and provide feedback

8. Generate and test hypotheses

9. Use questions, cues, and advance organizers (Dean et al., 2012, as cited in Marzano, 2003, p. 80)

While these strategies do not represent the only way to respond to learning, they do offer a researched and informed approach that may be different from how teachers taught the skills and concepts the first time. As teams discuss additional ways to re-engage student thinking at the conceptual level, these strategies allow for the critical thinking necessary for learning to occur.

Identify Similarities and Differences

This instructional strategy asks students to compare, contrast, and classify using thinking maps, graphic organizers, or Venn diagrams. Teachers can also use metaphors and analogies as a way to recognize patterns and relationships among concepts. The key is that students clarify their thinking by analyzing, evaluating, generalizing, comparing, and reasoning to make connections. This strategy moves the learning from memorizing to thinking and from *what I don't understand* to *what I know*.

Summarize and Take Notes

In many classes, teachers expect students to take notes during instruction. Note-taking does not ensure learning. It might help students memorize information for a later assessment or deliver a large amount of content in a short time when slides are the mode of instruction. This type of instruction often takes *thinking* out of the process. It becomes a mundane way to cover material quickly. However, when we add *summarizing* the notes to the process, it becomes a thinking activity. When teachers ask students to synthesize information by reviewing their notes to determine the gist of the information into a twenty- to twenty-five-word summary of the most important information, then students are engaged in analyzing, reasoning, evaluating, generalizing, and making connections. Reviewing notes and summarizing details can be an effective way to re-engage student thinking during Tier 2 intervention.

Reinforce Effort and Provide Recognition

As discussed in chapter 4 (page 63), analyzing trends in student work allows for more targeted and specific interventions and also reinforces student effort as teachers point out what's good about a student's work and then support the student in moving his or her learning forward. When teachers use data in this manner, they develop a growth mindset in students (Dweck, 2006). Teachers must ensure students understand what they did well in their work. Praise or recogniztion that focuses just on how hard students work usually has a negative effect because struggling students will only hear that despite their hard work, they still were unable to reach proficiency. This means that effort must be tied to learning evidence, especially as teachers work to assist students who struggle to learn the first time. Students will look at Tier 2 interventions as a punishment or failure if teachers do not approach them with a growth mindset.

Recognizing effort applied to learning helps develop a growth mindset in both teachers and students. It is important for students to understand the relationship between effort and learning. A powerful way to help students make this connection is to ask them to track their efforts and achievement side by side using a simple one-to-four rubrics or scale. This encourages productive struggle.

Provide Homework and Practice

Homework is a hot topic with teachers, students, and parents. Traditionally, teachers assigned homework to give students enough practice to deepen their learning. However, who actually does the work and whether students complete homework assignments are variables often too difficult to control. Many teachers also spend an inordinate amount of time trying to collect homework.

Since practice is so important to learning, as teams plan a unit of instruction, they should include a sufficient amount of time for students to practice the most essential learning targets in class. When many students need Tier 2 interventions, teams need to ask how much actual practice they provided to ensure learning, and whether they relied on practice outside of actual class time to accomplish this.

There are many ways to provide practice in Tier 2 interventions. (In chapter 6 on page 95, we address the specifics of how to provide schedules that include time during the school day to implement Tier 2 interventions.) Usually, teams group students with like or similar needs together to re-engage their thinking. Then, students can practice with partners or small groups, or with games that reinforce a skill. There are increasingly more ways to utilize technology to provide the necessary practice and reinforcement that deepen learning.

Encourage Nonlinguistic Representation

Nonlinguistic representation is a valuable strategy for Tier 2 interventions. This process asks students to make learning visible or audible. Students generate mental pictures of their learning. This is an opportunity for students to demonstrate their learning in pictures by using graphic organizers or constructing models. Students can use graphic organizers to depict a sequence of events, cause-and-effect relationships, or generalizations and patterns. Teachers often use this strategy to help students learn vocabulary through clues and pictures. Students can use a variety of media to produce nonlinguistic representations such as drawings, audio, video, and presentations. This strategy requires students to use their reasoning, clarifying, interpreting, and creating skills.

Include Cooperative Learning

Cooperative learning has long been considered a process that promotes learning (Johnson & Johnson, 1999; Johnson, Johnson, & Holubec, 2008). Learning occurs through interaction with others, but ultimately students must master many concepts individually. Hattie (2012) states, "Learning is collaborative and requires dialogue, and this requires teachers to be attentive to all aspects of peer-to-peer construction and meditation" (p. 39). The tasks and expectations teachers assign to groups must be explicit and lend themselves to an analysis of individual student learning. Tier 2 interventions are based on individual student needs. As cooperative groups work, teachers must be able to assess individual needs as well as promote collaborative work. If teachers use cooperative groups in Tier 1 instruction, then they must be clear on how they will determine if each individual student has learned the essential standard or learning target.

Set Objectives and Provide Feedback

In chapter 4 (page 63), we emphasize the importance of students owning their learning. This is best accomplished when students partner with their teacher from the beginning of the unit—not just before the test. It all begins with understanding the learning targets or objectives for the unit. Students not only need to see the learning targets but also envision what good or proficient work looks like. They must clearly understand the target and be able to articulate what it means to achieve it.

During the learning process, students track their progress, learning target by learning target. Then when students struggle to learn, they can point out exactly what they do not understand. Tier 2 interventions become a regular part of instruction and the learning process rather than something separate from other learning.

During the learning process, feedback is an integral part of moving the learning forward. It is feedback, not grades, that truly impact learning (Butler, 1988; Wiliam, 2011). Receiving formative feedback along the way, not just at the end, is most powerful. It makes thinking apparent, as students share feedback with the teacher and their peers. Feedback should cause thinking, not an emotional response. Wiliam (2018) states:

> Feedback should be focused; it should relate to the learning goals that have been shared with the students; and it should be more work for the recipient than the donor. Indeed, the whole purpose of feedback should

be to increase the extent to which students are owners of their own
learning. (p. 153)

In Tier 2 interventions, teachers should provide scaffolds, supports, or feedback
that moves the learning forward. This means feedback is most effective using the
"less is more" strategy. Teachers give minimal or just enough feedback for student
to make progress. Additionally, if teachers give scaffolded feedback regularly, it feeds
learning in a positive way and should not elicit a negative or an emotional response.

In a study by University of Illinois psychology professor Jeanne D. Day and
Eastern Connecticut State University associate professor and psychology department
chair Luis A. Cordón (1993, as cited in Wiliam, 2011), students who received scaffolded responses and feedback learned more and retained their learning longer than
students given full solutions. When teachers provide complete solutions, it removes
the opportunity for student thinking and learning.

Dean and colleagues (2012) have four recommendations for classroom practice
with regard to providing feedback.

▽ Provide feedback that addresses what is correct and elaborates on
what students need to do next.

▽ Provide feedback appropriately in time to meet students' needs.

▽ Provide feedback that is criterion referenced.

▽ Engage students in the feedback process. (p. 11)

These recommendations are particularly important when delivering Tier 2
interventions. Through using feedback, both students and teachers learn. Feedback
provides specific, accurate information so teams can address the common misconceptions students demonstrate in a timely manner.

Generate and Test Hypotheses

This instructional strategy engages students in problem solving, investigating,
exploring, experimenting, inventing, testing, and making decisions as they complete
a task. This is higher-level thinking necessary for learning transfer and retention. An
example is asking students to read a short passage to determine the theme, and then
asking them to reread the same passage to find evidence, both stated and inferred, to
support their answer. This close reading activity requires students to make meaning of
the passage using previous knowledge and understanding, which strengthens learning. This close reading strategy requires inductive reasoning, which involves making
inferences based on knowledge that students already have or information contained
in the text to make meaning. Utilizing this strategy makes thinking apparent in
the lesson.

Tier 2 interventions should not focus merely on relearning a particular skill but on the thinking necessary to generalize the learning to new and novel situations. All students, even those who struggle, need to engage in high-level tasks that require complex thinking.

Use Questions, Cues, and Advance Organizers

Questions and *cues* are important Tier 2 strategies. Questions and cues serve the same purpose in a lesson. They both activate students' prior knowledge and give them an idea of what they will learn. If students can answer questions or respond to a cue with one or two words, these questions or cues generally elicit a rote or recall response. During instruction, it is necessary to ask a few questions that include simple answers. But in order to re-engage student thinking, questions must be more complex and open ended and require reasoning. Tier 2 interventions should include questioning, thinking, reasoning, and learning from both incorrect and correct answers. Teachers should expect students to justify and explain why an answer is correct or why it is incorrect. This requires thinking beyond the right or wrong answer choice.

Using *advance organizers* also connects new concepts to students' prior knowledge with items like K-W-L charts that ask students what they think they *know* about a topic, what they *want* to learn, and finally what they *learned* along the way (Ogle, 1986). There are many other types of advance or graphic organizers that promote thinking, such as time and sequence pattern organizers used to organize events in chronological order. Other examples include process organizers used to identify cause-and-effect relationships or patterns, generalizational pattern organizers used to make generalizations and add examples that support the generalizations, and descriptive pattern organizers used to describe a topic. All of these graphic representations or organizers promote thinking and help students monitor their understanding and comprehension.

It is important in Tier 2 interventions for teachers and students to reflect on what they've already learned and what they haven't learned yet. Rather than reteaching from the beginning, this type of reflection clarifies the specific area of focus and allows students to think about their learning and give feedback to the teacher regarding where they might be stuck.

Although each of these instructional strategies can be used in Tier 1 instruction or Tier 2 interventions, it is important to note that Tier 2 interventions should not be *more of the same.* Tier 2 interventions should include targeted instruction to address the specific misconceptions and missteps in the learning of individuals or small groups with like or similar needs. When planning a lesson, consider which of these strategies will work for initial instruction and which are suited to re-engaging thinking for students who need a little more help to learn the essential standards.

Extend Students Who Are Already Proficient

As teams answer the four PLC critical questions to guide their work on a unit-by-unit basis, the one question they often forget is, "How will we extend the learning for those who already know it?" (DuFour et al., p. 251). This is also apparent as teams plan Tier 2 interventions. An educational workshop participant once said, "I am most concerned about the students in my class who spend most of their time watching others learn" (personal communication, February 18, 2015). This statement should make all teachers think about those students who either know the information before the teacher introduces it or learn it quickly. These students exist in every classroom; many either tune out or just develop a sense of being ignored. Each student deserves to learn something every day, regardless of the apparent needs of struggling students.

It is clear that in too many classrooms, educators gear their whole-group instruction to the middle-level students and support those near the bottom. This approach usually means that approximately four to five students understand the lesson, while some are lost and trying to catch up. The others clearly understand the lesson and have stopped listening and thinking. If teams intentionally answer that fourth question prior to teaching the unit, teachers would have a plan for *all* students.

As teams plan for Tier 2 interventions, members often ask what the other students will do while teachers are providing the additional support for the students who need it? In other words, how do teachers differentiate so all students continue to learn? The real stumbling block with differentiation is teachers often think they need to write an additional whole unit of instruction at a higher level or teach the standards from the next grade level or honors class. Differentiation does not have to be that complex or require that much work or planning.

Consider a sixth-grade mathematics team that taught a unit on ratios and proportions and then administered a short two-problem assessment that included multistep word problems. The team analyzed the data to determine trends and misconceptions. It then grouped students according to its errors analysis for Tier 2 interventions.

The team next planned an extension activity on ratios and proportions that involved concepts and skills, along with critical thinking the teacher had not directly taught. The teacher asked students to write their own multistep word problems involving ratios and proportions with an answer equal to or less than twenty-five. The teacher told the students to be sure their word problems required thinking and reasoning since they would exchange papers with a partner after completing the problems. This is clearly an extension of what was taught but still involves a deep understanding of ratios and proportions. This small activity deepened student learning of the content. In addition, the teacher did not duplicate any materials, grade or score any papers, or develop a differentiated unit. The team merely planned for the students who already learned the essential standards.

In another example, the English team gave an assessment focused on determining the theme of a literary text and the supporting evidence. Just as in the mathematics example, the team administered a short five-question assessment on the unit essential standards. The English team examined the results to determine trends in student work and the types of errors students made. The team then grouped students by specific errors and misconceptions. These students were then assigned to groups to re-engage their thinking for a Tier 2 intervention.

The team planned an activity for the students who demonstrated proficiency on the assessment. The teachers asked these students to do a close read of a short story to determine how the author developed the theme throughout the text. They were to cite specific examples from the text that were either stated or inferred. When students finished this activity, they met in small groups to compare their thinking and deepen their understanding of theme.

Once again, this activity aligns with the essential standards in the unit but extends the thinking of the students who were already proficient. In this way, the teacher honors the learning of these students. And the teacher did not duplicate any materials, grade or score any papers, or develop a differentiated unit. The team merely planned for the students who already learned the essential standards.

The key point is, as teams are planning for interventions to give more time and support to students who have not learned the essential standards, they need to also plan what the other students will do. The activity must extend their learning, not be just *more of the same*. It must align with the unit standards and not require the team or any individual teacher to plan another whole lesson. It must be something the teacher did not directly teach in the instructional process. Keep it a simple activity, but one that demands higher-level thinking and reasoning to deepen the students' ability to generalize the concepts to new or novel situations.

Conclusion

Tier 2 interventions and extensions are really two sides of the same coin. Both are necessary because of the academic diversity in every classroom. Even in specialized classes such as advanced placement, students have of a wide range of prior knowledge and learning needs. To truly ensure learning for all, *all* has to really mean *all*.

The instructional strategies in this chapter offer several pathways to accomplish an all-inclusive learning environment where every student learns.

The "Chapter 5: Key Considerations Rubric" reproducibles on pages 93–94 serve as a touchstone for schools and teams to evaluate their current reality and inspire conversations regarding areas of strength for the team or school, areas to focus on, and next steps. Teams can use this simple rubric during team meetings or with the whole faculty as a way to foster discussions about implementing effective RTI in their school.

Big Ideas for Chapter 5

The following eight big ideas provide an overview of the most important concepts from this chapter.

1. The goal of both interventions and extensions is to re-engage student thinking at the conceptual level, deepen their understanding, and allow them to transfer generalized learning to new or novel situations.

2. One of the greatest challenges individual teachers and collaborative teams face is responding to the academic diversity in every classroom.

3. Instructional supports for interventions and extensions cannot be a repeat of the initial teaching only louder and slower.

4. Instruction should always honor student learning with respectful tasks.

5. Teams must proactively plan the instructional supports for Tier 2 intervention and extensions *before* teaching the unit.

6. Powerful instructional supports are research informed and offer suggestions for Tier 2 interventions.

7. Instructional supports must align with the specific learning needs of each individual student or small student groups with like misconceptions.

8. Extending the learning of students who demonstrate proficiency and higher-level knowledge is as important and necessary as providing supports for students who struggle to learn.

Chapter 5: Key Considerations Rubric

Directions: With your school or team, read the key considerations listed in the far-left column of the rubric. Evaluate where your team or school currently is and what steps you need to establish in your daily practice to achieve these goals. Once completed, with your team discuss your areas of strength, areas of challenge, and next steps for your school or team.

Embedded

This is how we do business. We do this without thinking about it; it's just part of our school or team culture.

Developing

We get it and do fairly well in implementing this into our daily work.

Limited

We have some individuals in our school or team who understand and implement this, but it's sporadic at best.

No Evidence

There is little to no evidence of this; we have work to do!

Key Considerations	Embedded	Developing	Limited	No Evidence
Teams are intentional in answering all four PLC critical questions on a unit-by-unit basis.				
Teams analyze data to determine trends and specific errors and misconceptions.				
Teams plan interventions and address the targeted needs of individual students and small groups with like or similar needs.				
Teams proactively plan both interventions and learning extensions.				

page 1 of 2

Key Considerations	Embedded	Developing	Limited	No Evidence
The interventions and extension activities at Tier 2 honor student learning with respectful tasks.				
Teams develop extension activities by including concepts the teacher has not taught directly and that require complex thinking.				
Teams utilize powerful, researched, informed strategies to ensure learning.				

An area of **strength** for us:

An area of **challenge** for us:

Our **next steps**:

page 2 of 2

Building Time in the Schedule for Additional Support

Will you act with a sense of urgency, as if the very lives of your students depend on your action, because in a very literal sense, more so than at any other time in American history, they do?

—Richard DuFour

A Story From Pleasant Valley Middle School

The sixth-grade team at Pleasant Valley Middle School was in the middle of its weekly collaboration time. Over the past few months, the team had engaged in some difficult, but clarifying work. Seeing the need to be clear on the essential standards from class to class, the team spent a lot of time coming to consensus on the absolute essential standards. This was difficult work, as each team member brought a different perspective to the work and as a result, each valued very different essential standards.

Through its conversations, the team soon discovered students were receiving very different educational experiences in the same course simply because each teacher on the team placed different curricular priority on what students needed to know based on the teacher's personal experiences and perspectives. One teacher summed it up the best, "Two students can grow up right next door to each other, go to the very same schools, and yet have a wildly different educational experience in our language arts classes based on which teacher they have and what that teacher values." These critical team conversations led to a sense of urgency in gaining consensus on what *all* students need to know and be able to do in the course.

These conversations moved the team members to action. They spent hours gaining collective clarity on the essential standards and unpacking them into assessable learning targets. Following this, the team engaged in deep conversations about what it would accept as proficiency on the essential standards and targets; in other words, they addressed the question, What will a student know and be able to do when he or she is proficient?

Once the team was clear on the essential standards and targets, team members found developing common formative assessments a natural next step. The team developed and collectively administered assessments, which provided specific data regarding which students were proficient in the targeted area and which needed extra time and support.

However, the energy the team felt in getting to this level of instruction and assessment clarity soon changed. The question on each team member's mind was simple, "Now what? Even after our very best initial instruction, we still have targeted students who require extra time and support." As team members considered the school's current structure and bell schedule, they realized they didn't have time built into the school day to respond to the targeted students.

The sixth-grade team in this scenario engaged in the critical work of giving curricular priority to certain standards and deconstructing those essential standards to a level that each team member understands. Team members are clear on what they expect from the students in their classes to demonstrate proficiency. Along with this valuable work, the team also developed assessments to give to all students and met to review them as a team. Make no mistake, this is commendable work! Like many teams, the sixth-grade team at Pleasant Valley Middle School now needs additional time during the school day to provide the support for the students who need it.

This chapter will explain *why* we need to do things differently when building time in the schedule for additional support and offer specific strategies and tools for *how* to get there.

Why We Need to Do Things Differently

The challenge facing the sixth-grade Sunnyside team is one most teams and schools will need to address as they work toward ensuring all students learn at high levels. Most school structures are built around the idea of teachers delivering the curriculum to students. Consider the all-too-common discussions in schools and districts that focus on which bell schedule to use during the year—a block or traditional schedule—and choosing between options like a four-period block, five-period block, or traditional seven-period day.

Although these discussions are important, often they focus on the wrong idea. Instead of focusing on which schedule allows more time for teachers to deliver content, teams should focus on answering the question, Which structure will provide teachers with the necessary instructional time as well as extra time and support for students who need it?

We are not familiar with any research that strongly affirms one bell schedule or structure over another. We have seen a variety of different structures and bell schedules that provide both quality Tier 1 instructional time *and* time for extra support for students who require it. In short, the team conversation should not focus on which bell schedule allows teachers to deliver the most curriculum, but instead on how the team can build a schedule that provides time for quality instruction *and* adequate support for students who need extra time to learn the essential standards and targeted skills *during the school day*. When schools engage in conversations about bell schedules and structure in a school, the following four questions can help guide their thinking.

1. Does our schedule allow adequate time for targeted Tier 2 support (for teachers and students) or do teachers tell students to come before or after school for help?

2. What adjustments do we need to make to build flexible time into our daily schedule?

3. What does our schedule need to look like in order to provide quality Tier 1 instruction *and* adequate time for students who need extra targeted support?

4. How much time do our teams need to provide targeted Tier 2 intervention during the school day?

It's important to note these conversations are critical as the school moves from a focus on teachers delivering content to a focus on the team ensuring students have the necessary time to learn at high levels. As stated previously, we are not aware of one schedule or structure that works for every school. Instead, there are example after example of teams that have wrestled with these questions and found a schedule that works for their schools. These shared conversations help create ownership within the staff and school and are critical for schools as they move forward in providing extra time and support for students who require it.

Here's How

To provide effective interventions, some non-negotiable structures should be in place in each school. These structures allow for a schoolwide approach to supporting the learning of *all* students and provide a foundation for the school in which each educator is contributing to learning success for all students. These structures include:

▽ Universal screening system

▽ Bell schedule or structure that provides flexible time for interventions

▽ Effective intervention team

This section also offers some examples of school structures that address the need for creating flexible time within the school day. Keep in mind that there is no structure or schedule that works for all schools.

Universal Screening System

A schoolwide universal screening system that provides feedback to teachers and staff regarding each student's learning levels is a critical structure for schools. Buffum et al. (2009) define a *universal screening system* as:

> A process of reviewing student performance through formal and/or informal assessment measures to determine progress in relation to student benchmarks and learning standards; also, the practice of assessing all students in a school with valid measures in the major curricular areas, so that no student at risk "falls through the cracks." (p. 212)

Simply put, schools need a quick, efficient way to screen students and determine their functioning levels in the core learning skills of reading, writing, and mathematics. This system can be especially useful as students transfer from another school inside or outside the district and transition to next grade level. Think of this universal screening system as a quick check of a student's learning through, for example, reading scores, end-of-grade-level results, and writing samples. They don't need to be complex, time-consuming assessments. Consider this example of what administrators might ask a new student checking in at a new school:

> *"Welcome to our school! While your parent completes the required registration information, we'd like for you to tell us about your last school. Will you write a short paragraph about what you liked about your last school?"*

This quick writing sample allows educators to evaluate a student's writing and quickly assess if he or she appears to be on grade level or requires immediate support. Keep in mind that this is not an in-depth writing assessment but a simple general check to evaluate if the student is roughly at grade level.

It is also critical for schools to develop a coordinated system at each grade level that transfers meaningful learning data to help teachers immediately respond to a student's needs. Organizing this data into a universal screening system makes it less likely a student will fall through the cracks. Critical targeted learning information, such as reading level, writing level, and effective supports for students, are essential as schools establish a schedule for students and supports that teachers can implement immediately without losing valuable instructional time.

Figure 6.1 shows an example of general information that teacher and intervention teams can obtain about a new student using a universal screening system.

Student Name	Reading	Writing	Mathematics
James Arturo	The student must read aloud a short, grade-level reading passage.	The student must write a reponse to a simple writing prompt such as: Tell us the three things you hope to accomplish at school this year.	The student must solve two to three grade-level mathematics problems.
Evaluation	⬭At grade level⬭ Approaching grade level Below grade level	At grade level Approaching grade level ⬭Below grade level⬭	⬭At grade level⬭ Approaching grade level Below grade level
Next Steps		Notify language arts team and intervention team.	

Figure 6.1: Example of universal screening system.

In this example, the student is at grade level in reading and mathematics but scored below grade level in writing. In this case, a member of the leadership team would notify the student's teachers, the language arts team, and the intervention team about the concern, and these teams would create a targeted intervention to immediately address the cause for concern. A simple screener like this example can help a school identify general causes for concern and allow the school to immediately begin the extra time and support needed for the student.

Bell Schedule or Structure That Provides Flexible Time for Intervention

If schools are to provide time and support for struggling students, it is essential to have flexible time for teacher teams to support those who need it built into the daily schedule, regardless of the school's established schedule.

The important thing to remember is that teams must do the work of clarifying what *all* students need to know and then develop a way to commonly assess student proficiency in these areas. Teams then use the assessment results to identify which students need extra time and support in the targeted areas. From this, the school collectively develops a structure to provide extra time and support for struggling students within the school day.

As teams and schools consider Tier 2 intervention structures, they should remember certain essential elements. The following six-step process from *Taking Action: A Handbook for RTI at Work* (Buffum et al., 2018) will help schools target their conversations and help teams become more concise in thinking about and implementing effective Tier 2 interventions.

1. **Identify concerns:** Common formative assessments targeted on specific skills are critical for teacher teams to answer specific questions about student learning and team members' teaching practices. They help identify any concerns and need for improvement and intervention. Using assessment results, teams can engage in discussions about students who were unsuccessful as well as look for patterns in group performance to discover what might be affecting the group as a whole. This can also lead to discussions about the effectiveness of assessment construction.

   Teams and schools ask the question, "Do we have a process for identifying those students who require extra assistance?"

2. **Determine the cause:** Teacher teams may use common formative assessments results, as well as other streams of evidence, to determine the cause for some students not mastering essential standards. Teams should place these students into various intervention groups based on their targeted needs. For example, one group might require assistance in identifying a theme or central idea of a text, while another group might require assistance with using text details to identify the theme.

   Teams and schools ask the question, "Can we determine the specific needs of those students who require extra assistance?"

3. **Target the desired outcome:** Teams then make collective decisions about exactly what they want each group to be able to achieve as a result of the targeted intervention (the outcome). Focusing on what the student will be able to do (or what constitutes proficiency) allows teams to focus their efforts on providing the necessary time and support needed for students to achieve the proficiency expectation.

   Teams and schools ask the question, "What exactly do we want students to be able to do as a result of this intervention?"

4. **Design intervention steps:** Next, teams discuss potential strategies for each targeted intervention group. Oftentimes, teachers will use the results of the common formative assessments to compare the practices of each teacher. This is not a comparison of teachers, but instead, their practices for initial instruction. Engaging in this professional dialogue focused on which teaching practice elicited the best results fosters a sense of professional collegiality and, in turn, helps teams identify best practices for Tier 2 interventions.

   Teams and schools ask the question, "What Tier 2 supports can we create to provide targeted intervention for students?"

5. **Monitor progress:** Teams then decide which tools to use to monitor students' progress and eventual success. If developed with specific targets in mind, the common formative assessment allows teams to gather the information they need to intervene and monitor the success of the intervention correctly (Buffum et al., 2018). Once students master the learning target (or need), students should move out of the Tier 2 supplemental intervention.

Teams and schools ask the question, "Do we have systems in place to monitor the progress of students in our Tier 2 supplemental interventions?"

6. **Assign lead responsibility:** Finally, teams determine which team (or staff) member is best prepared to provide the targeted intervention. It is useful for teams to consider if a team or staff member has training in this particular area, which member's practice elicited the best results, and which member could be trained on the essential standard in order to provide the intervention.

Teams and schools ask the questions, "Who is the most qualified and best prepared on the staff to provide the intervention?"

Effective Intervention Team

Most schools have some variation of an intervention team. Effective intervention teams are composed of education professionals tasked with ensuring students have the support they need to learn at high levels. These professionals may include counselors, the school psychologist, the speech and language pathologist, special education teachers, subject specialists, instructional aides, and possibly an attendance secretary.

Effective intervention teams meet weekly. Members identify the most appropriate response for a struggling student and then monitor the effectiveness of the intervention. One of the challenges an intervention team faces is effectively utilizing its limited intervention meeting time. Often, well-intentioned intervention teams spend a great deal of time sharing anecdotal stories about each student. Although sharing these stories is sometimes necessary, more often than not they take an abundance of valuable time from the goal of coordinating effective, targeted support for students.

Addressing the questions in figure 6.2 (page 102) will help intervention teams be more productive during their team meetings.

Once teams and schools gain clarity on the needed interventions, it is essential for them to build structures to support flexible time for learning within the daily schedule. These supports are critical not only to support student needs but also for teacher teams to have the time necessary to help all students. The following

Intervention Team Questions

Intervention teams meet each week to discuss students' academic and behavior supports. Addressing the following questions will help members identify the cause and provide targeted time and support.

1. **Symptom:** In three sentences or less, what specifically is happening with the student?

2. **Cause:** What is the root cause?

3. **Target:** In reviewing our school's system of interventions, what is the targeted intervention we will use to support this student?

4. **Monitor:** Who will be responsible for monitoring the impact of the intervention?

5. **Communication:** What specific information do we need to share with teachers to keep them informed of extra support provided?

6. **Re-evaluate:** Did the intervention work after one to two weeks? If not, what is the next targeted intervention we will use to support this student?

Source: © 2019 by Sunrise Ridge Intermediate School. Used with permission.

Figure 6.2: Intervention team questions.

*Visit **go.SolutionTree.com/RTIatWork** for a free reproducible version of this figure.*

secondary school examples describe schools that have built highly successful Tier 2 supplemental structures.

Secondary School Structure Examples

As you consider each of these examples, you will recognize similarities in each school's approach but also identify unique elements for what works at each school.

Flexible Time Built Into a Traditional Schedule

Fossil Ridge Intermediate School has approximately nine hundred sixth and seventh graders. Fossil Ridge uses a traditional seven-period schedule, and students attend every class on their schedule each day (see figure 6.3). Class periods are forty-nine minutes, with a three-minute passing time between classes. The school built thirty-four minutes into its daily schedule for Tier 2 support of targeted students. They call this time REACH (Reinforce, Extend, Achieve, Challenge, Help) to reflect the work they engage in with students during this period.

First Lunch		Second Lunch	
Period	**Time**	**Period**	**Time**
Announcements	7:45–7:48 a.m. (three minutes)	Announcements	7:45–7:48 a.m. (three minutes)
First	7:48–8:37 a.m. (forty-nine minutes)	First	7:48–8:37 a.m. (forty-nine minutes)
Second	8:40–9:29 a.m. (forty-nine minutes)	Second	8:40–9:29 a.m. (forty-nine minutes)
Third	9:32–10:21 a.m. (forty-nine minutes)	Third	9:32–10:21 a.m. (forty-nine minutes)
First Lunch	10:21–10:49 a.m. (twenty-eight minutes)	Fourth	10:24–11:13 a.m. (forty-nine minutes)
Fourth	10:49–11:38 a.m. (forty-nine minutes)	Second Lunch	11:13–11:41 a.m. (twenty-eight minutes)
Fifth	11:41 a.m.–12:30 p.m. (forty-nine minutes)	Fifth	11:41 a.m.–12:30 p.m. (forty-nine minutes)
REACH	12:34–1:08 p.m. (thirty-four minutes)	REACH	12:34–1:08 p.m. (thirty-four minutes)
Sixth	1:11–2:00 p.m. (forty-nine minutes)	Sixth	1:11–2:00 p.m. (forty-nine minutes)

Source: © 2017 by Fossil Ridge Intermediate School. Used with permission.

Figure 6.3: Example of flexible time built into a traditional schedule.

Teacher teams are absolutely clear on what all students need to know (or the essential standards and targets for each course and unit of instruction). Once the team achieved clarity, members discussed what proficiency would look like and how it would assess the essential standards and learning targets. From there, teams developed their common formative assessments. Teachers then go to their classrooms and teach the essential standards and learning targets using whichever instructional strategy they choose. The team members then administer the agreed-on short common formative assessment.

Following this, the team holds a collaboration meeting and collectively reviews the results of the common formative assessment data. These data are critical for the team to review; the data provide critical information on student learning and each teacher's chosen instructional strategy. Specifically, the team looks at the data and begins to address the following three questions.

1. Which students are proficient according to the criteria the team set?

2. Which students need additional time and support?

3. Which teaching practices elicited the best results?

Answering these questions is essential for the team as it provides critical feedback regarding student learning, support needed, and which teaching practices provide the best results. During this collaborative time, teams also use the data to decide who is best suited to reteach the concepts. These conversations are essential for identifying the very best practitioners to ensure all students learn at high levels.

During these collaboration meetings, teams also identify the specific skills or concepts (based on the common formative assessment data) they will concentrate on during intervention time (REACH).

The team then sends its intervention offerings to an administrative assistant in the main office, who compiles them into a master schoolwide intervention offering for the upcoming two weeks. The offering changes every two weeks but aligns with the team's agreed-on pacing guide. Teams post offerings for each REACH time on the school's website and post hard copies around the school so students know what offerings are available during each two-week period.

Teams group students according to the essential standards and targeted needs by utilizing *student planners* (handbooks that include a daily calendar of the school year). Fossil Ridge requires students to carry their planners at all times, and each teacher has an ink stamp indicating *Intervention required*. The teacher places a stamp in a student's planner on the day the student must attend the targeted intervention. Teams assign students to the teacher they identified as most effective in teaching a particular concept based on the results of the common formative assessments and collaboration meeting. Teachers direct all students with a stamp in any of the deficient concept areas to the session that focuses on their specific concept needs.

For example, after a two-week unit of instruction focusing on adding and subtracting integers, a mathematics team would conduct a collectively developed assessment to determine proficiency. The team asks five questions ranging in complexity in each area (adding integers and subtracting integers) for a total of ten questions on the common assessment. The team has also made the collective decision that a student would need to score at least a four of five in each section to be proficient. Once the team administers the common formative assessment, members come together to review the assessment. They sort students as proficient and nonproficient in each of the assessed areas. The team then discusses who is the best candidate to reteach adding integers and who is best to reteach subtracting integers. (Ideally, they are the teachers whose students demonstrated the best results on the assessment.) Those teachers then get the names of students who will be in their intervention class.

At the conclusion of an intervention session, the teacher gives a short reassessment that focuses on the essential standards or learning target he or she retaught. If proficient, a student's new score replaces the existing score in the teacher's gradebook. If the student does not demonstrate proficiency after two attempts, the teacher refers the student to a more intense, targeted intervention. This is often a Tier 3 intervention that focuses specifically on the student's need. This process continues until the student demonstrates a sufficient level of proficiency in the concept or skill, as agreed on by the intervention team.

Flexible Time Built Into a Middle School Schedule

Desert Hills Middle School has approximately one thousand eighth- and ninth-grade students. The school uses a four-period schedule and students attend eight classes on alternating days (periods one through four on day A and periods five through eight on day B). Class periods are seventy-five minutes, with a four-minute passing time between classes (see figure 6.4). The school has built twenty-nine minutes into its daily schedule for Tier 2 support of targeted students. It has two lunches, one for ninth graders and one for eighth graders. While the ninth graders are at lunch, the eighth graders receive intervention support (homeroom) and vice versa during eighth-grade lunch.

Periods 1 and 5	8:25–9:40 a.m. (seventy-five minutes)
Periods 2 and 6	9:44–10:59 a.m. (seventy-five minutes)
Ninth-Grade Lunch Eighth-Grade Homeroom Support	10:50–11:28 a.m. (twenty-nine minutes)
Announcements	11:28–11:36 a.m. (eight minutes)
Eighth-Grade Lunch Ninth-Grade Homeroom Support	11:36 a.m.–12:01 p.m. (twenty-nine minutes)
Periods 3 and 7	12:05–1:20 p.m. (seventy-five minutes)
Periods 4 and 8	1:24–2:39 p.m. (seventy-five minutes)

Source: © 2017 by Desert Hills Middle School. Used with permission.

Figure 6.4: Example of flexible time built into a middle school schedule.

One of Desert Hills's Tier 2 targeted interventions is its homeroom support structure. Teacher teams first reached consensus on which essential standards and learning targets are critical for students to know and be able to do within the course and unit of instruction. Team use agreed-on common formative assessments to determine which students need extra time and support in each targeted area. Each unit of instruction is about two to three weeks long.

On Mondays, each student in the school receives a missing assignment report. This report serves as a reminder to the student about the work he or she is expected to perform during the provided support time. All students receive extra time to work on current or missing assignments with the support of a classroom teacher for twenty-nine minutes each day.

During their dedicated collaboration time, teacher teams determine the answers to the following three questions:

1. Which students need extra time and support on an essential standard or learning target?

2. Which team member will provide the targeted intervention?

3. What additional assistance or resources do teachers need to provide that support?

Teams identify and direct students requiring extra time and Tier 2 support to their assigned intervention by giving them intervention request passes. These identified students then receive targeted support on the essential standards or learning targets in which they weren't proficient. At the end of the homeroom support period, teams give students a short reassessment to determine if they are proficient or require additional support. This homeroom support period provides teachers and students with an additional twenty-nine minutes per day to engage in Tier 2 targeted interventions.

Flexible Time Built Into a Four-Period Block Schedule

Hurricane High School has approximately one thousand tenth-, eleventh-, and twelfth-grade students. The school uses a four-period schedule and students attend eight classes on alternating days (periods 1–4 on day A and periods 5–8 on day B). Class periods are seventy-five minutes, with a five-minute passing time between classes (see figure 6.5). Each Monday, the school adjusts the schedule to provide teachers with a one-hour collaborative session so they can plan for the coming week's interventions. Notice that the schedule and class period duration are different on Monday as compared to Tuesday through Friday. On Tuesday through Friday, the school built thirty minutes into their daily schedule for Tier 2 support of targeted students.

During their collaboration meeting, content teams first create a curriculum map. The map has a calendared sequence of lessons for the entire school year. All members of the team commit to follow the map.

Next, the content teams decide what standards are the *need to knows* or essential content of the course. These are the standards every student must master. The team will provide interventions for students who do not demonstrate mastery of these standards.

Content teams then create common formative assessments for each unit that emphasize the essential content from each unit. All team members commit to administer the same common formative assessments and compare data. (The district has already created these for secondary mathematics 1, 2, and 3.)

Schedule	Monday	Tuesday	Wednesday	Thursday	Friday
8:10–9:25 a.m.	First period	First period	First period	First period	First period
9:25–9:30 a.m.	Passing period	Passing period	Passing period	Passing period	Passing period
9:30–10:00 a.m.	Second period	Intervention	Intervention	Intervention	Intervention
10:00–10:05 a.m.		Passing period	Passing period	Passing period	Passing period
10:05–10:45 a.m.		Second period	Second period	Second period	Second period
10:45–11:20 a.m.	Lunch				
11:20–11:25 a.m.					
11:25–11:30 a.m		Lunch	Lunch	Lunch	Lunch
11:30 a.m.–12:00 p.m.	Third period				
12:00–12:05 p.m.					
12:05–12:45 p.m.		Third period	Third period	Third period	Third period
12:45–12:50 p.m.	Passing period				
12:50–1:20 p.m.	Fourth period				
1:20–1:25 p.m.		Passing period	Passing period	Passing period	Passing period
1:25–2:05 p.m.		Fourth period	Fourth period	Fourth period	Fourth period
2:05–2:10 p.m.					
2:10–2:40 p.m.	Teacher collaboration				
2:40–3:10 p.m.					

Source: © 2017 by Hurricane High School. Used with permission.

Figure 6.5: Example of flexible time built into a four-period block schedule.

The schedule is arranged to accommodate Tier 2 interventions. The Tier 2 interventions must be timely, directive, based on the essential standards, and identify the cause and student. There are two causes for nonproficiency.

1. Lack of will or insufficient effort

2. Lack of skill, understanding, or ability

At the high school level, teams are small and teachers cover multiple subjects. For example, a social studies teacher might teach U.S. history, world history, and government (multiple preps). Thus, the availability of daily Tier 2 interventions is necessary to provide frequent access to students who need intervention.

Tagging is the process of identifying which students do not show proficiency on the content standard and are thus identified by their teacher teams during their collaboration time. These students are selected to receive Tier 2 intervention.

Priority Tagging

The *tagger* is a shared spreadsheet with every student listed on the main page. Once a teacher "tags" a student, the teacher's name shows up next to the student's name so other teachers are aware that this student has been identified for intervention. The tagger allows teams throughout the school to see which students have been identified for extra time and support.

Priority Days

As some students will be tagged by multiple teams for extra time and support, the teams establish *priority days*. Priority days allow teams who have tagged a student to have preference on that particular day. For example, if a student has been tagged by both the science and mathematics team, this student would attend science intervention on Wednesday (priority day) and mathematics on Thursday (priority day). Designated priority days are as follows.

▽ Tuesday: Language arts

▽ Wednesday: Science

▽ Thursday: Mathematics

▽ Friday: Social studies and electives

Free Tagging

In order to provide additional opportunities for teams to provide students with extra time and support, teams developed *free tagging*. Using the tagger, teams may tag any student who has not been tagged for intervention after 2:40 p.m. on Monday.

Monday Collaboration Meeting

As stated earlier, Monday's schedule differs from Tuesday through Friday's schedule. On Monday, the schedule provides one hour at the conclusion of the school day for teams to discuss their common formative assessments, identify which students will be tagged, and determine which team member would be best to reteach during the intervention times on Tuesday through Friday. Guidelines for Monday's collaboration meeting are as follows:

▽ Content teams review data from common formative assessments to determine what essential skills and knowledge need to be retaught and which students need that reteaching.

▽ Before 2:40 p.m., content teams tag the students they have identified as needing intervention on the shared tagger document.

▽ After 2:40 p.m., content teams then review their students' learning on any specific essential standard. Teams may then decide to tag additional students to attend intervention.

Intervention Roles

On any intervention schedule, schools should maximize the time they have with targeted intervention. It is essential for schools to clearly define roles and expectations of staff to ensure intervention time is as productive as possible. The roles for intervention are as follows.

Teacher teams:

▽ Identify students who are nonproficient in a given essential standard or learning target.

▽ Tag the students requiring extra time and support on specific essential standards using the tagger.

▽ Identify which teacher is best to provide the intervention.

▽ Tag any additional students who could use extra assistance during the free tagging period (Mondays after 2:40 p.m.).

Administrators:

▽ Oversee the clerical component of the intervention process.

▽ Monitor hallways during the intervention period.

▽ Ensure that interventions are taking place through frequent visits to classrooms during the intervention period.

▽ May optionally provide a Tier 2 behavioral intervention.

Counselors:

▽ Provide a closed intervention for students whose behavior is preventing them from learning.

Incentives and Consequences

There are consequences and incentives involved in attending or missing assigned interventions, including the following consequences and incentives. As part of the process, Hurricane High implemented incentives for those who choose to follow the expectations of the intervention time. For those who demonstrate responsibility and consistently take advantage of the extra learning time, the school offers the opportunity to go to lunch early on Friday. Students who choose otherwise will be deemed ineligible to participate in extra-curricular activities.

Flexible Time Built Into a High School Schedule

Brownsboro High School has 820 ninth-, tenth-, eleventh-, and twelfth-grade students. The school uses an eight-period schedule and students attend eight classes on each day. Class periods are forty-five minutes, with a four-minute passing time between classes. The school has built thirty minutes into their daily schedule for Tier 2 support and enrichment of targeted students. Teachers may assign students to classrooms based on deficiencies in essential skills (see figure 6.6).

Period	Time
1	8:00–8:45 a.m.
2	8:49–9:34 a.m.
Enrichment	9:38–10:11 a.m.
3	10:15–11:00 a.m.
Lunch A	11:00–11:30 a.m.
4	11:34 a.m.–12:19 p.m.
5	12:23–1:08 p.m.
4	11:04–11:49 a.m.
Lunch B	11:49 a.m.–12:19 p.m.
5	12:23–1:08 p.m.
4	11:04–11:49 a.m.
5	11:53 a.m.–12:38 p.m.
Lunch C	12:38–1:08 p.m.
6	1:12–1:57 p.m.
7	2:01–2:46 p.m.
8	2:50–3:35 p.m.

Source: © 2019 by Brownsboro High School. Used with permission.

Figure 6.6: Bell schedule for student enrichment.

If not assigned, students may choose any open room (see figure 6.7). Teams track the enrichment period through a shared Google doc. The class offerings change weekly based on student needs, and each student receives a new schedule every Monday indicating where he or she should go each day (if assigned).

Examples of Tier 2 Supplemental Support

Along with structures that support Tier 2 intervention, schools and teams should carefully identify and consider the causes for a student's success in class. As discussed in chapter 2, a critical first step is for schools and teams to identify what is preventing each student from learning at high levels. Once identified, schools can

Subject	Room Number	Teacher	Week of February 5				
Language Arts	C122	Herring	AP writing		AP writing		Social studies tutorials
Mathematics	A105	Goodman	Open: homework help in mathematics	Open: mathematics		Open: mathematics	Open: mathematics
	A107	Potter		Open: algebra 1, geometry		Open: algebra 1, geometry	
	A108	Heideman	Open: precalculus help	Open: Texas Success Initiative (TSI) help (helping students for entrance exam into junior college)		Open: algebra 2, TSI, precalculus help	Open: algebra 2, TSI, precalculus help
	A117	Bacchari	Open: algebra 2, TSI help	Open: algebra 2, TSI help	Open: algebra 2, TSI help	Open: algebra 2, TSI help	
	A118	Nicholsen	Open: dual credit, calculus help	Open: dual credit, calculus help		Open: dual credit, calculus help	Open: dual credit, calculus help
	A119	Benson				Open: geometry, end-of-course homework help	Open: geometry, end-of-course homework help
	A120	Dunford		Open: algebra 1 homework help			Open: algebra 1 homework help
	C114	Jackson	Open: algebra 1 homework help	Open: algebra 1 homework help	Open: algebra 1 homework help	Open: algebra 1 homework help	Open: algebra 1 homework help

Figure 6.7: Schedule for student choice of supports.   continued →

Subject	Room Number	Teacher	Week of February 5				
Science	D117	Little					
	D124	Florence	AP biology retests, pre-lab help	Freshmen homework help	AP biology retests, pre-lab help	University Interscholastic League (UIL) practice	UIL practice
	D126	Rogers					
	D127	Curley		Retests: Students attend this intervention to retake a test that they didn't do well on or missed.	Missing work	Missing work	
	D128	Simon	Targeted homework: punnett square	Missing homework	Freshman biology genetics	Closed	Missing homework
	D132	Peterson	Chemistry re-quizzes	Missing work: analysis practice set 2	Closed	Missing work: analysis practice set 1	Chemistry makeup, lab and physics help

Source: © 2019 by Brownsboro High School. Used with permission.

design Tier 2 supplemental interventions to support students in the areas they are struggling. For example, if a student is having difficulty with a class because he or she just can't find assignments and homework in the "black hole" of his or her backpack, a likely Tier 2 intervention might focus on organizational skills. Once the student demonstrates the ability to organize and submit homework in a timely fashion, he or she would exit the intervention.

The following are examples of common Tier 2 supplemental supports schools offer that specifically target student needs.

▽ **Preteaching concepts or vocabulary:** Schools may choose to identify students who typically struggle with new concepts. Teachers could then provide students time within the school's schedule for preteaching upcoming concepts, big ideas, and vocabulary. The goal is for students to be better prepared with a preview of upcoming learning and building background knowledge that will assist them as they learn new content.

▽ **Flexible learning time:** For students who need a little extra time to master a concept, schools can provide extended learning time for teachers and students. Often referred to as *flex time*, schools create an extra block of time during the school day for students to receive targeted help in specific areas. Teams utilize their common formative assessment data to determine which students need additional time and support to learn key concepts.

Remember, teachers should not use flexible time to repeat content instruction. Instead, they should use flex time to present ideas for targeted support. Of utmost importance is for schools and teams to identify what is preventing students from learning at high levels and then create ways to provide targeted support for students in those areas.

▽ **Guided homework:** For students who have a difficult time completing their homework, schools may provide a time for guided homework. Guided homework places students in a smaller setting with support from a staff member who works to ensure these students complete the assigned homework.

▽ **Basic organization skills:** Often, a student struggles in a class or course due to lack of organizational skills. The student understands the content, yet lacks the basic organizational skills needed to manage the multiple secondary school classes. You will recognize these types of students, as their backpacks are places where assignments and homework enter, never to be found again. These students struggle in class not because they don't understand the content but because they can't find the assignment or homework or simply forget to turn in their work. Providing these students with targeted support in basic organizational skills will help them function better in the classroom.

▽ **Extended learning time:** Schools often have hidden chunks of time they can repurpose to provide extra learning for students. For example, at Fossil Ridge Intermediate School, the leadership team examined its current schedule searching for extra time for learning. The leadership team discovered their school had a tradition of providing twenty minutes per day for *silent sustained reading* (SSR). The leadership team examined this block of time and soon realized it could use the twenty minutes for SSR as well as for targeted extending learning time for students who needed support in mathematics. So, the leadership team identified and placed students who needed extra time in a mathematics class followed by SSR. Instead of reading during the designated SSR time, these students received additional time and targeted instruction on essential mathematics skills. The leadership team discovered that a simple adjustment provided an extra twenty minutes a day for students who needed extra time and support. Over the 180-day school year, this added up to more than sixty hours of additional support through extended learning time.

Conclusion

As schools consider ways to provide Tier 2 time and support, keep in mind that there is not a one-size-fits-all structure for implementing the RTI process. Instead, schools should be creative in their approaches to designing a bell schedule and structure that support teachers and students. The examples shared in this chapter are the result of committed, creative schools utilizing the resources they have available to them. Each of the schools featured have two things in common: (1) it has created a structure that works for their needs, and (2) the structure is the result of many ideas, numerous attempts, and inevitably, committed educators who are determined to find a structure that provides the necessary time and support needed for teachers and students.

The "Chapter 6: Key Considerations Rubric" reproducibles on pages 116–117 serve as a touchstone for schools and teams to evaluate their current reality and inspire conversations regarding areas of strength for the team or school, areas to focus on, and next steps. Teams can use this simple rubric during team meetings or with the whole faculty as a way to foster discussions about implementing effective RTI in their school.

Big Ideas for Chapter 6

The following three big ideas provide an overview of the most important concepts from this chapter.

1. All schools in the examples have the following three things in common.

   a. They did the work of identifying targeted areas of needed support for students.

   b. They built flexible time into their existing bell schedules for supplemental (Tier 2) interventions.

   c. They were creative in developing structures and schedules that support quality Tier 2 schoolwide support. Each found something that worked specifically for their school.

2. Flexible time within the school schedule is essential for providing Tier 2 support.

3. As schools design interventions, it's essential to engage in targeted conversations about the following.

   - Identify concern.

   - Determine the cause.

   - Target the desired outcome.

   - Design intervention steps.

   - Monitor progress.

   - Assign a team (or staff member) to be responsible for monitoring the effectiveness of the intervention.

Chapter 6: Key Considerations Rubric

Directions: With your school or team, read the key considerations listed in the far-left column of the rubric. Evaluate where your team or school currently is and what steps you need to establish in your daily practice to achieve these goals. Once completed, with your team discuss your areas of strength, areas of challenge, and next steps for your school or team.

Embedded

This is how we do business. We do this without thinking about it; it's just part of our school or team culture.

Developing

We get it and do fairly well in implementing this into our daily work.

Limited

We have some individuals in our school or team who understand and implement this, but it's sporadic at best.

No Evidence

There is little to no evidence of this; we have work to do!

Key Considerations	Embedded	Developing	Limited	No Evidence
Teams have flexible time built into their daily schedule to provide additional time and support for students who need it.				
Teams use intervention time to provide additional time and support on essential standards or learning targets for students who need it.				
Teams are clear on which students need assistance on essential standards or learning targets.				
The school structure supports student learning and not simply teachers delivering the curriculum.				

page 1 of 2

An area of **strength** for us:

An area of **challenge** for us:

Our **next steps**:

page 2 of 2

Epilogue

Do not wait; the time will never be "just right." Start where you stand, and work with whatever tools you may have at your command, and better tools will be found as you go along.

—George Herbert

A Story From Taft High School

The eleventh-grade science team at Taft High School had a dilemma. All team members had read numerous articles and publications about the power of PLCs and the effectiveness of RTI in ensuring *all* students learn at high levels. Each article they shared, book they read, and training they attended seemed to make sense. They were convinced they had to make a change to how their team and school supported students who needed extra assistance to succeed.

They believed their team and school needed to have Tier 2 supports in place, including processes for identifying students who needed supplemental help and determining their specific needs. The team was also confident it needed to develop structures and strategies for supporting these students as well as ways to monitor the effectiveness of its Tier 2 supplemental intervention efforts. But this is where collective efficacy stopped and the dilemma set in. Simply put, the team just didn't know where to start.

A few team members were convinced they needed a checklist of items to complete. Strict compliance to a checklist of items the team needed to do was the answer to their dilemma. While the team agreed there were certain elements of the checklist idea that made sense, the idea of strict compliance to a checklist seemed authoritarian.

A few team members suggested they begin by asking the principal to adjust the school's bell schedule and possibly overall structure of the daily routines embedded since the turn of the 20th century. To them, a change to the school's bell schedule seemed to be where to start.

The remaining team members thought they just needed to get greater clarity on the standards, especially those collectively deemed essential, followed by revisiting their common formative assessments to determine if they were assessing the essential skills.

Hence, the team's dilemma. Where was the right place to begin?

It's important to remember, in this wonderful world of education, we are all learning. The learning part of a PLC is directed at us, the educators who have chosen learning as our career. You are going to make mistakes, it's inevitable! As legendary UCLA basketball coach John Wooden (n.d.) once said, "The team that makes the most mistakes usually wins, because doers make mistakes."

So, with your team, make a personal commitment to be doers. There is certainly not one way to develop a perfect Tier 2 system. Schools around the world have discovered new and exciting ways to meet the learning needs of all their students. What separates them from other schools is simple; they have a desire to keep experimenting until they find interventions that work, as long as their efforts focus on student learning.

To help with your journey, we want to review certain essential, foundational elements that teams and schools need to make part of their journey in developing effective Tier 2 supplemental supports for students.

▽ **Clarify what students need to know and be able to do:** In order for schools to build effective Tier 2 supplemental supports, teams must engage in the work of identifying what students need to know and be able to do in each course or class. Using the standards as a foundation, teams need to get what author Mike Mattos (2016) calls, "insanely clear on what students need to know and be able to do." This includes teams getting together and doing the work of giving curricular priority to certain standards. Once teams have identified the essential standards, they then begin the process of breaking down the standard into measurable targets and having conversations about ways to commonly assess these targets and skills. Again, teams will not be able to develop effective Tier 2 interventions and supports until they are absolutely clear on what skills and behavior require interventions.

▽ **Develop common formative assessments that align with the essential standards:** Once teams are clear on the essential standards and targets, it is critical that their common formative assessments align with these targets, contain the level of rigor needed to meet the targets, and utilize the results to determine which students are proficient and which students need extra time and support to meet the target proficiency. These assessments are more than just a score in the gradebook, but serve as a diagnostic tool for student learning.

▽ **Identify causes for student struggles:** Essential to building an effective Tier 2 system of interventions, schools and teams need to identify the root cause for student struggles. Schools must engage in deep, meaningful conversations about the things preventing students from learning at high levels. Once schools identify the causes for student struggles, they can begin to evaluate their current Tier 2 supports to determine if they are effective in addressing causes for these struggles. If the school identifies causes for student struggles their Tier 2 supports do not address, teams can then engage in a conversation about what a Tier 2 intervention would look like to provide the necessary support.

▽ **Build a bell schedule that supports learning:** As schools consider a system of interventions, an essential initial step is to examine their current bell schedule and determine if it is built to simply deliver curriculum or ensure *all* students have the time and support to learn at high levels.

▽ **Monitor the effectiveness of interventions:** Intervention structures are common in today's schools. It is common to visit a school and see a smattering of offerings described as interventions. What is uncommon is for schools and teams to be consistently revisiting their interventions and determining if each intervention is effective in meeting the needs of students who need more time and targeted support. Schools and teams must be consistently assessing the effectiveness of their interventions to determine if they are having the desired effect; that is, Is the intervention providing targeted time and support to help each student learn at high levels?

Ensuring *all* students learn at high levels is tough . . . but so are you! Like you, when we chose to enter the teaching profession, it was for something greater than money or fame. Instead, we entered this profession for a more compelling purpose—to make a difference in the lives of students who enter our schools and classrooms each day. We are confident that as your school and collaborative teams identify what is preventing your students from learning at high levels and create strategic Tier 2 supplemental structures and supports, your students, teachers, and school will come ever closer to achieving the goal of ensuring high levels of learning for every student. We wish you the very best on your journey!

References and Resources

Ainsworth, L. (2003). *Power standards: Identifying the standards that matter the most*. Englewood, CO: Advanced Learning Press.

Ainsworth, L. (2010). *Rigorous curriculum design: How to create curricular units of study that align standards, instruction, and assessment*. Englewood, CO: Lead + Learn Press.

Ainsworth, L. (2013). *Prioritizing the Common Core: Identifying specific standards to emphasize the most*. Englewood, CO: Lead + Learn Press.

AZQuotes. (n.d.). *Margot Fonteyn quotes*. Accessed at www.azquotes.com/author/4969-Margot _Fonteyn on February 20, 2017.

Bailey, K., & Jakicic, C. (2012). *Common formative assessment: A toolkit for Professional Learning Communities at Work*. Bloomington, IN: Solution Tree Press.

Bailey, M. J., & Dynarski, S. M. (2011). *Gains and gaps: Changing inequality in U.S. college entry and completion* (NBER Working Paper No. 17633). Cambridge, MA: National Bureau of Economic Research.

Balu, R., Zhu, P., Doolittle, F., Schiller, E., Jenkins, J., & Gersten, R. (2015). *Evaluation of response to intervention practices for elementary school reading*. Washington, DC: National Center for Education Evaluation and Regional Assistance. Accessed at https://ies.ed.gov/ncee /pubs/20164000/pdf/20164000.pdf on February 24, 2017.

Barber, M., Chijioke, C., & Mourshed, M. (2010). *How the world's most improved school systems keep getting better*. Accessed at www.mckinsey.com/industries/social-sector/our-insights/how-the -worlds-most-improved-school-systems-keep-getting-better on February 24, 2017.

Barber, M., & Mourshed, M. (2007). *How the world's best-performing school systems come out on top*. Accessed at http://mckinseyonsociety.com/how-the-worlds-best-performing-schools-come-out-on -top on February 24, 2017.

Brantlinger, E. A. (Ed.). (2006). *Who benefits from special education? Remediating (fixing) other people's children*. Mahwah, NJ: Erlbaum.

Breslow, J. M. (2012, September 21). *By the numbers: Dropping out of high school*. Accessed at www.pbs.org/wgbh/frontline/article/by-the-numbers-dropping-out-of-high-school on February 24, 2017.

Buffum, A., & Mattos, M. (2015). *It's about time: Planning interventions and extensions in elementary school*. Bloomington, IN: Solution Tree Press.

Buffum, A., Mattos, M., & Malone, J. (2018). *Taking action: A handbook for RTI at Work*. Bloomington, IN: Solution Tree Press.

Buffum, A., Mattos, M., & Weber, C. (2009). *Pyramid response to intervention: RTI, professional learning communities, and how to respond when kids don't learn.* Bloomington, IN: Solution Tree Press.

Buffum, A., Mattos, M., & Weber, C. (2012). *Simplifying response to intervention: Four essential guiding principles.* Bloomington, IN: Solution Tree Press.

Burns, M. K., Appleton, J. J., & Stehouwer, J. D. (2005). Meta-analytic review of responsiveness-to-intervention research: Examining field-based and research-implemented models. *Journal of Psychoeducational Assessment, 23*(4), 381–394.

Butler, R. (1988). Enhancing and undermining intrinsic motivation: The effects of task-involving and ego-involving evaluation on interest and performance. *British Journal of Educational Psychology, 58*(1), 1–14.

Chappuis, J., Stiggins, R., Chappuis, S., & Arter, J. (2012). *Classroom assessment for student learning: Doing it right—using it well* (2nd ed.). Boston: Pearson.

Cleveland Clinic. (n.d.). *The very best way to lose weight and keep it off.* Accessed at https://my.clevelandclinic.org/health/articles/4662-the-very-best-way-to-lose-weight--keep-it-off on November 15, 2018.

Conzemius, A. E., & O'Neill, J. (2014). *The handbook for SMART school teams: Revitalizing best practices for collaboration* (2nd ed.). Bloomington, IN: Solution Tree Press.

Covey, S. R. (1989). *The seven habits of highly effective people: Powerful lessons in personal change.* New York: Fireside.

Day, J. D., & Cordón, L. A. (1993). Static and dynamic measures of ability: An experimental comparison. *Journal of Educational Psychology, 85*(1), 75–82.

Dean, C. B., Hubbell, E. R., Pitler, H., & Stone, B. (2012). *Classroom instruction that works: Research-based strategies for increasing student achievement* (2nd ed.). Alexandria, VA: Association for Supervision and Curriculum Development.

Diament, M. (2014, April 29). Graduation rates fall short for students with disabilities. *Disability Scoop.* Accessed at www.disabilityscoop.com/2014/04/29/graduation-rates-disabilities/19317 on December 17, 2015.

Donovan, M. S., & Cross, C. T. (Eds.). (2002). *Minority students in special and gifted education.* Washington, DC: National Academies Press.

DuFour, R. (2015). *In praise of American educators: And how they can become even better.* Bloomington, IN: Solution Tree Press.

DuFour, R. (2016). *Advocates for professional learning communities: Finding common ground in education reform.* Accessed at www.allthingsplc.info/files/uploads/AdvocatesforPLCs-Updated11-9-15.pdf on February 27, 2017.

DuFour, R., DuFour, R., Eaker, R., & Many, T. W. (2006). *Learning by doing: A handbook for Professional Learning Communities at Work* (1st ed.). Bloomington, IN: Solution Tree Press.

DuFour, R., DuFour, R., Eaker, R., Many, T. W., & Mattos, M. (2016). *Learning by doing: A handbook for Professional Learning Communities at Work* (3rd ed.). Bloomington, IN: Solution Tree Press.

DuFour, R., & Eaker, R. (1998). *Professional Learning Communities at Work: Best practices for enhancing student achievement.* Bloomington, IN: Solution Tree Press.

Dweck, C. S. (2006). *Mindset: The new psychology of success.* New York: Ballantine.

Education for All Handicapped Children Act of 1975, Pub. L. No. 94–142, 20 U.S.C. § 1401 (1975).

Ferri, B. A., & Connor, D. J. (2006). *Reading resistance: Discourses of exclusion in desegregation and inclusion debates*. New York: Lang.

Fisher, D., & Frey, N. (2014). *Checking for understanding: Formative assessment techniques for your classroom* (2nd ed.). Alexandria, VA: Association for Supervision and Curriculum Development.

Francis, E. (2016). *What exactly is the depth of knowledge?* Accessed at http://edge.ascd.org/blogpost /what-exactly-is-depth-of-knowledge-hint-its-not-a-wheel on March 23, 2019.

Fulton, K., & Britton, T. (2011). *STEM teachers in professional learning communities: From good teachers to great teaching*. Washington, DC: National Commission on Teaching and America's Future.

Gallagher, K. (2009). *Readicide: How schools are killing reading and what you can do about it.* Portland, ME: Stenhouse Publishers.

Gewertz, C. (24 January, 2019). U.S. high school grad rate reaches another all-time high. But what does that mean? [blog post]. *Education Week.* Accessed at http://blogs.edweek.org/edweek/high _school_and_beyond/2019/01/2017_high_school_graduation_rate.html on March 26, 2019.

Gladwell, M. (2002). *The tipping point: How little things can make a big difference*. Boston: Back Bay Books.

Goodreads. (n.d.). *Benjamin Franklin quotes.* Accessed at www.goodreads.com/quotes/247269-an -ounce-of-prevention-is-worth-a-pound-of-cure on January 2, 2019.

Goodwin, M. (2009). Matchmaker, matchmaker write me a test. In T. R. Guskey (Ed.), *The teacher as assessment leader* (pp.89–110). Bloomington, IN: Solution Tree Press.

Hargreaves, A., & Fullan, M. (2012). *Professional capital: Transforming teaching in every school*. New York: Teachers College Press.

Hattie, J. (2009). *Visible learning: A synthesis of over 800 meta-analyses relating to achievement*. New York: Routledge.

Hattie, J. (2012). *Visible learning for teachers: Maximizing impact on learning*. New York: Routledge.

Hattie, J. (2018). *Hattie ranking: 252 influences and effect sizes related to student achievement.* Accessed at https://visible-learning.org/hattie-ranking-influences-effect-sizes-learning-achievement on March 22, 2019.

Individuals With Disabilities Education Improvement Act of 2004, 20 U.S.C. § 1400 *et. seq.* (2004).

Johnson, D. W., & Johnson R. T. (1999). *Learning together and alone: Cooperative, competitive, and individualistic learning*. (5th ed.). Boston: Allyn and Bacon.

Johnson, D. W., Johnson R. T., & Holubec, E. J. (2008). *Cooperation in the classroom* (8th ed.). Edina, MN: Interaction Book.

Kanold, T. D. (Ed.). (2015a). *Beyond the Common Core: A handbook for Mathematics in a PLC at Work, grades 6–8*. Bloomington, IN: Solution Tree Press.

Kanold, T. D. (Ed.). (2015b). *Beyond the Common Core: A handbook for Mathematics in a PLC at Work, grades K–5*. Bloomington, IN: Solution Tree Press.

Kanold, T. D. (Ed.). (2015c). *Beyond the Common Core: A handbook for Mathematics in a PLC at Work, high school*. Bloomington, IN: Solution Tree Press.

Kanold, T. D. (Ed.). (2015d). *Beyond the Common Core: A handbook for Mathematics in a PLC at Work, leader's guide*. Bloomington, IN: Solution Tree Press.

Kramer, S. V. (2014). *Connecting the dots: From essential outcomes to assessment to interventions and enrichment*. Presented at PLC at Work Institute, June 17, 2014. Orlando, Florida.

Kramer, S. V., & Schuhl, S. (2017). *School improvement for all: A how-to guide for doing the right work*. Bloomington, IN: Solution Tree Press.

Mader, J., & Butrymowicz, S. (2014, October 29). For many with disabilities, special education leads to jail. *Disability Scoop*. Accessed at www.disabilityscoop.com/2014/10/29/for-sped-leads-jail/19800 on January 26, 2016.

Marzano, R. J. (2003). *What works in schools: Translating research into action.* Alexandria, VA: Association for Supervision and Curriculum Development.

Marzano, R. J. (2007). *The art and science of teaching: A comprehensive framework for effective instruction.* Alexandria, VA: Association for Supervision and Curriculum Development.

Marzano, R. J. (2010). *Formative assessment and standards-based grading.* Bloomington, IN: Marzano Resources.

Marzano, R. J. (2017). *The new art and science of teaching.* Bloomington, IN: Solution Tree Press.

Marzano, R. J., Pickering, D. J., & Pollock, J. E. (2001). *Classroom instruction that works: Research-based strategies for increasing student achievement.* Alexandria, VA: Association for Supervision and Curriculum Development.

Mattos, M. (2016). *Mike Mattos on how to get insanely clear on learning outcomes and learning objectives.* Accessed at www.youtube.com/watch?v=SL_50Sf_7eY on August 30, 2016.

Mense, E., & Crain-Dorough, M. (2017). *Data leadership for k–12 schools in a time of accountability.* Hershey, PA: IGI Global.

Moss, C. M. & Brookhart, S. M. (2009). *Advancing formative assessment in every classroom: A guide for instructional leaders.* Alexandria, VA: Association for Supervision and Curriculum Development.

National Governors Association Center for Best Practices & Council of Chief State School Officers. (2010a). *Common Core State Standards for English language arts and literacy in history/social studies, science, and technical subjects.* Washington, DC: Author. Accessed at www.corestandards.org/assets/CCSSI_ELA%20Standards.pdf on January 3, 2018.

National Governors Association Center for Best Practices & Council of Chief State School Officers. (2010b). *Common Core State Standards for mathematics.* Washington, DC: Author. Accessed at www.corestandards.org/assets/CCSSI_Math%20Standards.pdf on January 3, 2018.

No Child Left Behind Act of 2001, Pub. L. No. 107–110, 20 U.S.C. § 6319 (2002).

Popham, W. J. (2003). *Test better, teach better: The instructional role of assessment.* Alexandria, VA: Association for Supervision and Curriculum Development.

Popham, W. J. (2011). *Transformative assessment in action: An inside look at applying the process.* Alexandria, VA: Association for Supervision and Curriculum Development.

Prasse, D. P. (n.d.). *Why adopt an RTI model?* Accessed at www.rtinetwork.org/learn/what/whyrti on February 24, 2017.

Reardon, S. F. (2011). The widening academic achievement gap between the rich and the poor: New evidence and possible explanations. In G. J. Duncan & R. J. Murnane (Eds.), *Whither opportunity? Rising inequality, schools, and children's life chances* (pp. 91–116). New York: Sage Foundation.

Reeves, D. (2002). *The leader's guide to standards: A blueprint for educational equity and excellence.* San Francisco: Jossey-Bass.

Reeves, D. (2016). *FAST grading: A guide to implementing best practices.* Bloomington, IN: Solution Tree Press.

Rumberger, R. W. (2011) *Dropping out: Why students drop out of high school and what can be done about it.* Cambridge, MA: Harvard University Press.

Samuels, C. A. (2010). Learning-disabled enrollment dips after long climb. *Education Week, 30*(3), 1, 14–15.

Scherer, M., (2001) How and why standards can improve student achievement: A conversation with Robert J. Marzano. *Educational Leadership, 59*(1), 14–18.

Schmoker, M. (2004). Learning communities at the crossroads: Toward the best schools we've ever had. *Phi Delta Kappan, 86*(1), 84–88.

Schuhl, S. (2017). *Analyzing formative assessment student work products.* Response to Intervention Institute Presentation. May 10, 2017. New Orleans, LA.

Skiba, R. J., Poloni-Staudinger, L., Gallini, S., Simmons, A. B., & Feggins-Azziz, R. (2006). Disparate access: The disproportionality of African American students with disabilities across educational environments. *Exceptional Children, 72*(4), 411–424.

Skiba, R. J., Simmons, A. B., Ritter, S., Gibb, A. C., Rausch, M. K., Cuadrado, J., et al. (2008). Achieving equity in special education: History, status, and current challenges. *Exceptional Children, 74*(3), 264–288.

Sparks, S. D. (2015). Study: RTI practice falls short of promise. *Education Week, 35*(12), 1, 12.

Stiggins, R., Arter, J. A., Chappuis, J., & Chappuis, S. (2006). *Classroom assessment for student learning: Doing it right—Using it well.* Upper Saddle River, NJ: Pearson Education.

Tavernise, S. (2012, February 9). Education gap grows between rich and poor, studies say. *New York Times.* Accessed at www.nytimes.com/2012/02/10/education/education-gap-grows-between-rich-and-poor-studies-show.html on February 10, 2012.

United States Department of Education. (2006). *28th annual report to Congress on the implementation of the Individuals With Disabilities Education Act.* Washington, DC: Office of Special Education Programs.

United States Department of Education. (2015, February 12). *U.S. high school graduation rate hits new record high.* Accessed at www.ed.gov/news/press-releases/us-high-school-graduation-rate-hits-new-record-high on November 13, 2018.

Vagle, N. D. (2015). *Design in five: Essential phases to engaging assessment practice.* Bloomington, IN: Solution Tree Press.

Waack, S. (2018). Hattie ranking: 252 influences and effect sizes related to student achievement. *Visible Learning.* Accessed at https://visible-learning.org/hattie-ranking-influences-effect-sizes-learning-achievement on January 2, 2019.

Wilhelm, T. (2011). A team approach to using student data. *Leadership, 40*(5), 26–28, 30, 38.

Wiliam, D. (2011). *Embedded formative assessment* (1st ed.). Bloomington, IN: Solution Tree Press.

Wiliam, D. (2018). *Embedded formative assessment* (2nd ed.). Bloomington, IN: Solution Tree Press.

Wooden, J. (n.d.). *Quotefancy.* Accessed at https://quotefancy.com/quote/845216/John-Wooden-The-team-that-makes-the-most-mistakes-usually-wins-because-doers-make on January 23, 2019.

Index

Best Practices at Tier 1
Daily Differentiation for Effective Instruction, Secondary
Gayle Gregory, Martha Kaufeldt, and Mike Mattos
Created specifically to target core instruction in grades 6–12, this book provides proven response to intervention strategies to differentiate instruction, engage students, increase success, and avoid additional interventions. Discover how to create a brain-friendly learning environment, shift processes to support collaboration, and more.
BKF651

Taking Action: A Handbook for RTI at Work™
Austin Buffum, Mike Mattos, and Janet Malone
This comprehensive implementation guide covers every element required to build a successful RTI at Work program in schools. The authors share step-by-step actions for implementing the essential elements, the tools needed to support implementation, and tips for engaging and supporting educators.
BKF684

It's About Time
Planning Interventions and Extensions in Secondary School
Mike Mattos and Austin Buffum
Carve out effective intervention and extension time at all three tiers of the RTI pyramid. Explore more than a dozen examples of creative and flexible scheduling, and gain access to tools you can use immediately to overcome implementation challenges.
BKF610

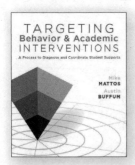

Targeting Behavior and Academic Interventions
A Process to Diagnose and Coordinate Student Supports
Mike Mattos and Austin Buffum
Students at risk of not acquiring essential academic skills also often experience behavior problems. With this unscripted video workshop, your team will learn how to use the Pro-Solve Process to determine the causes and potential solutions for students in need of interventions.
DVF072

WOW!

I liked how I was given
an effective, organized plan
to help EVERY child.

—Linda Rossiter, teacher,
Spring Creek Elementary School, Utah

 PD Services

Our experts draw from decades of research and their own experiences to bring you
practical strategies for providing timely, targeted interventions. You can choose from a
range of customizable services, from a one-day overview to a multiyear process.

Book your RTI PD today!
888.763.9045

Solution Tree